The Wisdom
of Business

The Wisdom of Business

....

A BOOK OF MAXIMS

Eugene Weber

ORION
BUSINESS
BOOKS

Copyright 1998 by Eugene Weber

Cartoons © 1998 by ~~Glasier~~

The right of Eugene Weber to be identified as the
author of this work has been asserted by him in accordance
with the Copyrights, Designs and Patents Act 1988

First published in Great Britain in 1998 by
Orion Business
An imprint of The Orion Publishing Group Ltd
Orion House, 5 Upper St Martin's Lane, London WC2H 9EA

A CIP catalogue record for this book
is available from the British Library.

ISBN 0-75281-398-6

Typeset by Selwood Systems, Midsomer Norton
Printed and bound in Great Britain by
Butler & Tanner Ltd, Frome and London

Contents

Accounting

●●●●●●●●●●●●●●●●●●●●●●●●●●●●●●●●●●●●

❝ I think of accounts like a haggis: if you knew what was in it, you wouldn't touch it with a barge pole. ❞

Professor David Tweedie, chairman of the Accounting Standards Board

Even rock stars eye their accountants with respect – or fear.
Stuart Crainer, management writer

A trademan's book, like a Christian's conscience, should always be clean and clear. And he that is not careful of both will give but a sad account of himself either to God or man.
Daniel Defoe, writer

Frequent accounting makes for lasting friendship.
Luca Pacioli, the creator of double entry bookkeeping

It is easier to teach a poet to read a balance sheet than it is to teach an accountant to write.
Henry Luce, publisher

Did you ever hear of a kid playing accountant – even if he wanted to be one?
Jackie Mason, comedian

An accountant is a man who puts his head in the past and backs his ass into the future.
Ross Johnson, former president of RJR Nabisco

He that gains well and spends well needs no account book.
George Herbert, poet

Achievement

●●●●●●●●●●●●●●●●●●●●●●●●●●●●●●●●●●●

❝ If you want to do something you
find a way. If you don't want to do
anything, you find an excuse. ❞

Arab saying

Nobody's perfect, but all of us can be better than we are.
Jackie Stewart, former racing driver

Nothing is ever achieved by reasonable men.
J Fred Bucy of Texas Instruments

To get anywhere in life you have to be anti-social.
Otherwise you'll end up being devoured.
Sean Connery, actor

Nothing comes from calm. Calm is boring.
Donatella Versace, fashion designer

There's so much more to be gained with honey, so much
more.
Lord Hanson, co-founder of Hanson plc

Ability is the art of getting credit for all the home runs
somebody else hits.
Casey Stengel, baseball manager

Resilience does not come overnight.
George Graham, football manager

Capitalism thrives on the right to be unequal, but it won't
survive unless everyone has the equal right to be unequal.
Professor Charles Handy, social philosopher

Advertising

●●●●●●●●●●●●●●●●●●●●●●●●●●●●●●●●●●

❝ ❝ Nudity or crude sexuality is
irrelevant, unless the product is a
brothel. ❞ ❞ *David Ogilvy, advertising guru*

A good ad should be like a good sermon; it must not only comfort the afflicted, it must also afflict the comfortable.
Bernice Fitz-Gibbon, retailer

Never write an advertisement which you wouldn't want your family to read.
David Ogilvy, advertising guru

When the client moans and sighs
Make his logo twice the size.
If he still should prove refractory
Show a picture of his factory.
Only in the gravest cases
Should you show the clients' faces.
Anonymous

Early to bed, early to rise; Never get tight and advertise.
Timothy Eaton, Canadian businessman

You must stir it up and stump it
And blow your own trumpet
Or trust me, you haven't a chance.
W S Gilbert, humorist

A good advertisement is one which sells the product without drawing attention to itself.
David Ogilvy, advertising guru

Word of mouth is the best medium of all.
William Bernbach, advertising executive

Make the layouts rough and the ideas fancy.
Stavros Cosmopulos, advertising executive

If you tell lies about a product, you will be found out – either by the government, which will prosecute you, or by the consumer, who will punish you by not buying your product a second time.
David Ogilvy, advertising guru

The first law in advertising is to avoid the concrete promise and cultivate the delightfully vague.
John Crosby, American advertising executive

Bad advertising can unsell a product.
David Ogilvy, advertising guru

We find that advertising works the way the grass grows. You can never see it, but every now and then you have to mow the lawn.
Andy Tarshis, of the A. C. Nielsen company

In advertising, to not be different is virtually suicidal.
William Bernbach, advertising executive

Regardless of the moral issue, dishonesty in advertising has proved very unprofitable.
Leo Burnett, American advertising executive

Advertising doesn't create a product advantage. It can only convey it.
William Bernbach, advertising executive

There is no such thing as 'soft sell' and 'hard sell'. There is only 'smart sell' and 'stupid sell'.
Charles Browder, former president of BBDO

Advertising in the final analysis should be news. If it is not news it is worthless.
Adolph S Ochs, newspaper publisher

What you say in advertising is more important than how you say it.
David Ogilvy, advertising guru

Advertising is the art of making whole lies out of half truths.
Edgar Shoaff, lawyer

Forget words like 'hard sell' and 'soft sell'. That will only confuse you. Just be sure your advertising is saying something with substance, something that will inform and serve the consumer, and be sure you are saying it like its never been said before.
William Bernbach, advertising executive

Advertisers who try to make social comments fall flat on their faces.
Gary Duckworth, planning director of Duckworth, Finn, Grubb, Waters

Two ads a day keep the sack away.
Saying among staff of Saatchi & Saatchi

The guy you've really got to reach with your advertising is the copywriter for your chief rival's advertising agency. If you can terrorise him, you've got it licked.
Howard Gossage, American advertising executive

If you call a spade a spade you won't last long in the advertising business.
Anon

The codfish lays ten thousand eggs,
the homely hen lays one.
The codfish never cackles
to tell you what she's done.
And so we scorn the codfish,
while the humble hen we prize,
which only goes to show you
that it pays to advertise.
Anon

If you have nothing to say, sing it.
David Ogilvy, advertising guru

Good wine needs no bush
and perhaps products that people really want need no
hard sell or soft sell tv push.
Why not?
Look at pot.
Ogden Nash, poet

The simplest way to assure sales is to keep changing the
product – the market for new things is infinitely elastic.
One of the fundamental purposes of advertising, styling
and research is to foster a healthy dissatisfaction.
Charles Kettering, former president at General Motors

Many people buy a product in spite of its advertising, not
because of it.
Rena Bartos, marketing executive

Agencies need to be kept slightly understaffed and slightly
overworked, and an occasional bout of disciplined panic
and 'ghosting' [working through the night] is no bad thing.
Peter Mayle, former advertising creative director

Agencies don't become rich and famous because of their
impeccable administrative procedures, or even their
financial acumen but because one or two people at the top
have been able to hold together a collection of wildly
conflicting personalities and motivate them into working
with each other. It is not a skill that can be learned
mechanically, but a knack, rather like being good with
animals.
Peter Mayle, former advertising creative director

Today it is almost an axiom that in order to discover the
truth of an advertisement it is necessary to read between
the lies.
Frank Irving Fletcher, copywriter

If you build a lousy mousetrap and spend $10,000,000 advertising it, the world will beat a path to your door.
Elmer Zilch, journalist

Nothing is more fragile than an advertising fashion.
Stephen Fox, author

The display in the window has to be powerful. It must shock you and stop you in the street. It should be controversial, it should be theatre.
Anita Roddick, co-founder of The Body Shop

The man who whispers down a well
About the goods he has to sell
Will not make as many dollars
As the man who climbs the tree and hollers.
Lord Leverhulme, industrialist

Advice

●●●●●●●●●●●●●●●●●●●●●●●●●●●●●●●●●●

❝ Make three correct guesses consecutively and you will establish a reputation as an expert. ❞

Laurence J Peter, educationalist

No one wants advice – only corroboration.
John Steinbeck, novelist

A good man giving bad advice is more dangerous than a
nasty man giving bad advice.
Conor Cruise O'Brien, academic

Never trust the advice of a man in difficulties.
Anon

A good scare is worth more to a man than good advice.
Ed Howe, journalist

The best way to advise children is to find out what they
want and then advise them to do it.
Harry Truman, former American president

The art of giving advice is to make the recipient believe he
thought of it himself.
Frank Tyger

I always advise people never to give advice.
P G Wodehouse, writer

Tom's [Peters] latest message, you know the slogan: 'crazy
times call for crazy solutions'. Well, it's the dumbest thing
I ever heard.
Bob Waterman, co-author of In Search of Excellence *(with Tom
Peters)*

The prophet whose time has come no longer shocks. He
entertains.
Peter Drucker, management guru

The secret of being an effective guru is being able to
appropriate the phrases.
David James, journalist

The best servants of the people, like the best valets, must whisper unpleasant truths in the master's ear.
Walter Lippmann, journalist

The only thing worse than slavishly following management theory is ignoring it completely.
The Economist

There's an old boxing saying: Touch gloves, go back to your corner and protect yourself at all times.
George Walker, businessman and former boxer

Ambition

••••••••••••••••••••••••••••••••

❝ Make no little plans; they have no magic to stir men's blood and probably themselves will not be realised. Make big plans; aim high in hope and work, remembering that a noble, logical diagram once recorded, will not die. ❞ *Daniel H Burnham, architect*

Ah, but man's reach should exceed his grasp
Or what's a Heaven for?
Robert Browning, poet

Dreaming is zero value. I mean, anyone can dream.
Bill Gates, co-founder of Microsoft

Keep away from people who try to belittle your ambitions. Small people always do that. But the really great make you feel that you too can become great.
Mark Twain, writer

You've got a goal, I've got a goal. Now all we need is a football team.
Groucho Marx, actor

Always aim for the stars and you may hit the barn roof.
Una-Mary Parker, author

Who never climbed high, never fell low.
Thomas Fuller, writer

If you would hit the mark, you must aim a little above it. Every arrow that flies feels the attraction of earth.
H W Longfellow, poet

Banks

• •

❝ Make sure you get bankers to come to your office. And always keep 'em waiting. Hit 'em around the head a bit. Let 'em know who's boss. ❞ *Kerry Packer,*

Australian businessman

Have you ever watched a rugby football match when one of the players loses his trousers? They all immediately go into a scrum to make sure no one can see, while they produce another pair of pants. That's how bankers behave when they see a default.
A British banker

Banks must be treated with absolute respect. You never surprise them.
Craig McCaw, American businessman

Good bankers, like good tea, can only be appreciated when they are in hot water.
Jaffar Hussein, banker

If you don't have some bad loans you are not in business.
Paul Volcker, former boss of the Federal Reserve

If you are short, take a loan. Never ask for a small amount. Ask for what you need and always pay it back, the sooner the better.
Aristotle Onassis, shipping tycoon

In the banking world the secret is to be boring.
Luis Valls Taberner, Spanish banker

If you get things 99 per cent right in this business you get a knighthood. Get things 97 per cent right and you are fired.
Sir Brian Pearse, banker

To be conservative in banking is to be in banking for a thousand years. The day you are not conservative you cannot survive.
Edmond Safra, banker

The first rule of a central banker is to appear confusing. The second rule is not to be confused.
Surjeet Bhalla, economist

The trouble with most banks is that the man who writes the advertising is not the same guy who lends you the money.
Anon

A 'sound' banker, alas! is not one who foresees danger and avoids it, but one who, when he is ruined, is ruined in a conventional and orthodox way along with his fellows so that no one can really blame him.
J M Keynes, economist

Adventure is the life of commerce, but caution, I had almost said timidity, is the life of banking.
Walter Bagehot, economist

The requirements of a successful Governor of the Bank of England are the tact and skill of an ambassador and the guile of a Romanian horse thief.
Lord Lever, Labour politician

A banker has to be both a salesman and an analyst. If you let the credit men – the analysts – run the bank, you won't have any customers. If you let the salesman run the bank, you go bankrupt.
George S Moore, banker

Bully the weak and suck up to the strong – it's a widespread business principle and the banks exemplify it. Do you ever get the feeling that the bank would really just as soon not have you as a client? You're right. What the banks secretly long to do is shut up all their regional offices, fire the staff and settle into air conditioned rooms in the City (where else?) and play the game of 'restructuring'.
Alan Clark, MP

Basics

●●●●●●●●●●●●●●●●●●●●●●●●●●●●●●●●●

❝ The first skill a diplomat must learn is to be able to read confidential papers upside down when he walks into someone else's office. ❞ *Michael Shea,*

communications expert and former diplomat

The first thing to do is to arrange to be born in Paris ...
after that everything follows quite naturally.
Diana Vreeland, fashion editor

Do your business as if you are going to be examined by a
leading QC: take up a position where no one can get
behind you and never cut corners.
Peter Grant, former chairman of Sun Life

You can't do business with bad people and you can't get
hurt with good people. That's all there is to know.
Howard Sheperd, banker

Moderation in all things, especially in moderation.
Max Mosley, motor racing executive

Get your retaliation in first.
Willie John McBride, former rugby player

Always be nice to bankers. Always be nice to pension fund
managers. Always be nice to the media.
Lord Hanson, co-founder of Hanson

To be successful, keep looking tanned, live in an elegant
building (even if you're in the cellar), be seen in smart
restaurants (even if you nurse one drink) and if you borrow,
borrow big.
Aristotle Onassis, shipping tycoon

The priority in life is to keep an eye on the business and
not to get lured into the social high life being exhibited
around by the groupie-type poseurs who wish to be seen
with the new blue-eyed boy.
Alan Sugar, founder of Amstrad

Start off with four kids. Make sure they hate each other and can't play. Demonstrate to record companies the enormous potential of a band that can't play. Make it as hard as possible for the Press to see it. Insult your audience as much as possible and cultivate hatred.
Malcolm McLaren, rock impresario

Start with good people, lay out the rules, communicate with your employees, motivate them and reward them. If you do all these things effectively, you can't miss.
Lee Iacocca, former boss of Chrysler

First comes the shy wish. Then you must have the heart to have a dream. Then, you work. And work.
Estee Lauder, perfumer

It doesn't matter if the cat is black or white, as long as it catches the mouse.
Deng Xiaoping, Chinese politician

I am convinced that the more money a new business needs to begin with, the less chance it has of being a success.
Mark McCormack, sports agent

Do whatever seems important first. Some people talk about five-year plans, but with me it's more like five days.
Tiny Rowland, former boss of Lonrho

There are those who work all day, those who dream all day, and those who spend an hour dreaming before setting to work to fulfil those dreams. Go into the third category, because there's virtually no competition.
Steven Ross, former boss of Time Warner

The best way to launch an Italian restaurant is to have it raided because the Mafia eats there. Everybody knows they eat well.
Mario Puzo, writer

Hitch your wagon to a star; keep your nose to the
grindstone; put your shoulder to the wheel; keep an ear
to the ground; and watch the handwriting on the wall.
Herbert Prochnow, banker

Don't open a shop unless you know how to smile.
Jewish saying

At the start you don't have very much to lose and yet there
is no limit to how far you can grow.
Sir Clive Sinclair, inventor and businessman

The rules are there are no rules.
Aristotle Onassis, shipping tycoon

The trouble with the first-time entrepreneur is that he
doesn't know what he doesn't know. After a failure he
does know what he doesn't know and can beat the hell
out of people who still have to learn.
Don Valentine, venture capitalist

If you can dream it, you can do it.
Walt Disney, film producer

I have two rules – never do business with any country that
has green in its flag or where they don't wear overcoats.
Sir Benjamin Slade, company director

If you do things well, do them better. Be daring, be
different, be just.
Anita Roddick, co-founder of The Body Shop

Chop your own wood and it will warm you twice.
Saying

If principles can become dated, they are not principles.
Warren Buffett, investment guru

The readiness is all.
William Shakespeare, playwright

Mistrust first impulses. They are nearly always wrong.
Charles Maurice deTallyrand, diplomat

Observe the masses and do the opposite.
James Caan, headhunter

Be always sure you're right, and then go ahead.
Davy Crockett, king of the wild frontier who died at the Alamo

Take a chance. Columbus did.
Bud Collins, sports writer

First, make yourself a reputation for being a creative genius.
Second, surround yourself with partners who are better
than you are. Third, leave them to get on with it.
David Ogilvy, advertising guru

Be realistic – demand the impossible.
Student slogan during the 1968 Paris riots

When starting a business you need to be self-sacrificing.
It's a bit like starting out with a new lover – he needs to
be looked after and treated well. Otherwise you lose him.
Janet Reger, lingerie designer

BOB MAKES 'THE BIKE' TOO SIMPLE.

Everything should be made as simple as possible, but not simpler.
Albert Einstein, scientist

Bureaucracy

●●●●●●●●●●●●●●●●●●●●●●●●●●●●●●●●●●●●●

❝ I can't stand this proliferation of paperwork. It's useless to fight the forms. You've got to kill the people producing them. ❞ *Vladimir Kabaidze, manager in Russia in the pre-Glasnost era*

When in charge, ponder. When in trouble, delegate. When in doubt, mumble.
James Boren, president of the National Association of Bureaucrats

One way to make sure crime doesn't pay would be to let the government run it.
Ronald Reagan, former American president

The battle against red tape is a battle that is never won. There is always someone – often from the best of intentions – who wants to tie another knot.
John Major, MP and former British prime minister

The road to national poverty is paved with good regulations.
William Waldegrave, MP

Companies always have a tendency to add levels.
Sir John Harvey-Jones, former chairman of I.C.I.

If you want to make a bureaucrat tremble, show him a really determined woman.
Lady Margaret Thatcher, former British prime minister

Bureaucracy defends the status quo long after the quo has lost its status.
Laurence J Peter, educationalist

It's a poor bureaucrat who can't stall a good idea until even its sponsor is relieved to see it dead and buried.
Robert Townsend, author of Up the Organisation

The man who is denied the opportunity of taking the decisions of importance begins to regard as important the decisions he is allowed to take. He becomes fussy about filing, keen on seeing the pencils are sharpened, eager to ensure that the windows are open (or shut) and apt to use two or three different-coloured inks.
C Northcote Parkinson, writer

Economic success and dictatorships are inversely related.
George Soros, speculator

Consistency is the last refuge of the unimaginative.
Oscar Wilde, writer and wit

What the world needs is more love and less paperwork.
Pearl Bailey, singer

Business

• •

❝ The only sure thing is that in business there are no sure things. ❞

Akio Morita, former chairman and chief executive of Sony Corporation

Business is like bull-fighting. You can't be an amateur and you can't be old.
Sir Peter Parker, former chairman of British Rail

Business is always aggressive: sometimes you win, sometimes you fail, but you must be aggressive.
Wei Mingyi, chairman of China International Trust and Investment Corporation

Business is never complicated. It's about selling something for the highest price and having a satisfied customer.
Gerry Robinson, chairman of Granada

The basic rules of business are the same whatever it might be. The basic requirement is always common sense.
Sir Charles Clore, businessman

Think of your business as a pet dog. You can't stop feeding it, or stroking it or taking it for walks because you're in hard times. What's going to happen if you don't feed your dog is that it's going to drop dead.
Gerald Ratner, former chairman of Ratners

If there's nothing in it for shareholders, there's nothing in it for management.
Greg Hutchings, boss of Tomkins

The rule of business is how fast you can get your idea to market. Those whose systems do not allow them to move quickly are doomed.
Ken Tuchman, boss of Teletech

The principal purpose of a company is not to make a profit, full stop. It is to make a profit in order to continue to do things or make things and to do so ever better and more abundantly. Profit has to be a means to other ends rather than an end in itself.
Professor Charles Handy, social philosopher

The boring side of business is what makes it work.
Alan Sugar, founder of Amstrad

Keeping a little ahead of conditions is one of the secrets of business, the trailer seldom goes far.
Charles Schwab, steel magnate

Business has only two basic functions: marketing and innovation.
Peter Drucker, management guru

Business is Darwinism: only the fittest survive.
Robert Holmes á Court, Australian financier

Business, more than any other occupation, is a continual dealing with the future: it is a continual calculation, an instinctive exercise in foresight.
Henry Luce, founder of Time *and* Fortune *magazines*

Being good is good business.
Anita Roddick, co-founder of The Body Shop

In business, if you are persistent you normally arrive. It's the old tortoise and hare story.
Noel Lister, co-founder of MFI

The secret of business is knowing something that nobody else knows.
Aristotle Onassis, shipping tycoon

Business is often about killing your favourite children to allow others to succeed.
Sir John Harvey-Jones, former chairman of I.C.I.

A business must have a conscience as well as a counting house.
Sir Montague Burton, founder of the Burton Group

It is an immutable law of business that words are words, explanations are explanations, promises are promises – but only performance is reality.
Harold Geneen, former chief executive of ITT

Business is war.
Japanese proverb

Quarterly figures have nothing to do with running a business.
Akio Morita, former chairman and chief executive of Sony Corporation

If you are in business, you're in it to win. You might as well be in it boots and all. It's amazing how much fun you can get out of doing unpleasant things if you are in it up to your neck.
Robert Holmes á Court, Australian financier

Nobody ever went broke underestimating the taste of the British public.
Anon

Dinner lubricates business.
Samuel Johnson, man of letters

Organisations are like internal combustion engines. They are 30 per cent efficient and 70 per cent of their time is wasted. It just seems to happen naturally.
Sir Christopher Hogg, chairman of Allied Domecq

Business must be aristocratic. There must be a top and, if possible, the best man must get there.
Henry Luce, founder of Time *and* Fortune *magazines*

Of all business activities, 99 per cent are routine. They do not require management attention except in the aggregate.
Alfred P Sloan, former head of General Motors

The Invisible Hand, if it is to be found anywhere, is likely to be found picking the pockets of the poor.
Edward Nell, economist

Great businesses turn on a little pin.
Saying

You can't do business sitting on your arse.
Lord MacLaurin, former chairman of Tesco

A businessman who reads *Business Week* is lost to fame. One who reads Proust is marked for greatness.
John Kenneth Galbraith, economist

In this business you have to be an optimist. Maybe a skeptical optimist, but an optimist nonetheless.
Hugh Mumford, venture capitalist

Businesswomen

●●●●●●●●●●●●●●●●●●●●●●●●●●●●●●●●●●●●●●

❝ A woman in business has to look like a lady, act like a man and work like a dog. ❞ *Ann Gloag, managing director*

of Stagecoach

Behind every successful businesswoman there's a man without a chip on his shoulder.
Richard Ross, co-founder with Sophie Mirman of Sock Shop

Success means you're not viewed as a sexual, warm woman.
Anita Roddick, co-founder of The Body Shop

When a man kisses your hand, it must be smooth and beautiful.
Estee Lauder, perfumer

If one is rich and one's a woman, one can be quite misunderstood.
Katharine Graham, newspaper proprietor

Good businessmen don't underestimate women, but bad businessmen always do.
Eileen Mulligan, founder of Micromode Medical

It's very easy for a woman who is successful in business to lose sight of her womanhood and femininity. I always think of Margaret Thatcher as the prime example of that. The bigger the shoulder-pads, the worse they are.
Lynne Franks, PR consultant

I shrug my shoulders in desperation at women who moan at the lack of opportunities and then take two weeks off as a result of falling out with their boyfriends.
Sophie Mirman, co-founder of Sock Shop

Change

●●●●●●●●●●●●●●●●●●●●●●●●●●●●●●●●

❝ If you spend too much time worrying about how other people perceive you, you'll never break the rules. ❞ *John Sculley, former chief executive of Apple Corporation*

If it ain't broke, break it.
Richard Pascale, management guru

In the new digital economy, things are changing hourly and you have to be very adaptable, very flexible.
Kevin Kelly, Big Think guy at Wired *magazine.*

You can't teach an old dogma new tricks.
Dorothy Parker, American writer

If you want to preach a revolutionary message, wear a suit.
Nelson Mandela, president of South Africa

Chaos often breeds life, when order breeds habit.
Henry Brooks Adams, American historian

The real secret is to build an organisation that isn't afraid to make changes while it is still successful, before change becomes imperative for survival.
Lew Platt, chief executive of Hewlett-Packard

You must be in tune with the times and be prepared to break with tradition.
William M Agee, chairman of Bendix Corporation

Business, more than any other occupation, is a continual dealing with the future. It is a continual calculation, an instinctive exercise in foresight.
Henry Luce, founder of Time *and* Fortune *magazines*

After you've done a thing the same way for two years look it over carefully. After five years look at it with suspicion and after ten years throw it away and start all over again.
Alfred Edward Pearlman, American railroad executive

General Motors, Sears and IBM were the greatest companies in their industries – the best of the best in the world. These companies did not make gigantic mistakes. They were not led by stupid, inept people. The only real mistake they made was to keep doing whatever it was that had made them successful for a little too long.
Lew Platt, chief executive of Hewlett-Packard

Think job light. Accept change as a friend. And don't take yourself too seriously.
Tom Peters, management guru

In a startup company you basically throw out all assumptions every three weeks.
Scott McNealy, co-founder of Sun Microsystems

Change, or the prospect of change will frighten everybody.
Sir John Harvey-Jones, former chairman of I.C.I.

If you never move an inch, that is not movement, that is monument.
Mick McGahey, mining leader

If you see a bandwagon, it's too late.
Sir James Goldsmith, industrialist and politician

Never be a pioneer. It's better to be second or third.
Sir Mark Weinberg, company director

Restructuring is rather like planting asparagus. You know you should have started three years ago.
Charles M Doszher, company director

Start restructuring when things are going well and not when the water is already up to your neck.
Fritz Leutwiler, former chief executive of Brown Boveri & CIE

Innovation comes from creative destruction.
Yoshihisa Tabuchi, company director

Initiative is successful disobedience.
John Fenton, sales guru

Make sure you have a vice president in charge of
Revolution, to engender ferment among your more
conventional colleagues.
David Ogilvy, advertising guru

Every organisation has to prepare for the abandonment of
everything it does.
Peter Drucker, management guru

Don't talk about the latest significant restructuring.
Significant restructuring never stops.
Tom Peters, management guru

You can't go into a [football] club and tell people their
fitness is terrible, that they're bevvying, they're playing too
much golf, and their ground is filthy. You simply have to
improve things bit by bit.
Alex Ferguson, football manager

If a company gets too large, break it into smaller parts.
Once people start not knowing the people in the building
and it starts to become impersonal, it's time to break up
the company.
Richard Branson, founder of Virgin Group

The thing is to be able to outlast the trends.
Paul Anka, singer

People tend to think of the past as a hindrance. But you
can't have a revolution every day. The past also enables
and can be a dynamic force. It confers certain advantages
such as trust, brands, reputations and relationships.
Don Sull, business guru

Change alone is unchanging.
Heraclitus, 5th century philosopher

It is only the wisest and most stupid who cannot change.
Confucius, philosopher

If in the last few years you haven't discarded a major
opinion or acquired a new one, check your pulse. You may
be dead.
Gelett Burgess, writer and humorist

Oppose, adapt, adopt.
Benjamin Disraeli, statesman

There is a saying in football that if you stand still you go
backwards.
George Graham, football manager

Every revolution evaporates and leaves behind the slime
of a new bureaucracy.
Franz Kafka, writer

In our reforming zeal, we should not forget that old
institutions often embody wisdom which is temporarily
out of fashion.
William Waldegrave, MP

You either get better or you die. To stick in a groove is an
illness.
Leonard Bernstein, composer

Look abroad through Nature's range
Nature's mighty law is change.
Robert Burns, poet

He that will not apply new remedies must expect new evils,
for time is the greatest innovator.
Francis Bacon, philosopher

If you want to know about water, don't ask a fish.
Marshall McLuhan, communications guru

The art of progress is to preserve order amid change and preserve change amid order.
A N Whitehead, mathematician

Defending yesterday – that is, not innovating – is far more risky than making tomorrow.
Peter Drucker, management guru

Change is only another word for growth, another synonym for learning. We can all do it if we want to.
Professor Charles Handy, social philosopher

Even divergence deserves to be cherished, simply because it widens the bounds of life.
Kabel Caper, lawyer

There is a time to zig and a time to zag. There are times when companies should not just be bullied into doing things by the fad of the moment.
Jonathan Fry, company director

It is easier to resist at the beginning than at the end.
Leonardo da Vinci, artist

Organisations are rather like giant jellies. If you resculpt too limited a part of them they wobble back into their old form. But if you try to remould too much at once, the whole effort becomes unmanageable and they collapse in a quivering heap. The jelly may even become rock-solid and resistant to further shaping.
Richard Heygate, partner at McKinsey & Co

Communication

••••••••••••••••••••••••••••••••••••••

❝ Some people will believe anything
if it's whispered to them. ❞ *Anon*

Taking a mobile phone into the bedroom should be grounds for divorce.
Lord Deedes, journalist

If you can't convince them, confuse them.
Harry Truman, former American president

The spoken word is like a sped arrow that cannot be recalled.
Lord Mason, Labour politician

A speech is like a love affair. Any fool can start it, but to end it requires considerable skill.
Lord Mancroft, former civil servant

Speak comfortable words.
William Shakespeare, playwright

The ill and unfit choice of words wonderfully obstructs understanding.
Francis Bacon, philosopher

Tact is the ability to describe others as they see themselves.
Abraham Lincoln, American statesman

You impress folks that little bit more with what you are saying if you say it nicely. People don't hear your ideas if you just stand there shouting out words.
Lord Gormley, former miners' leader

Tart words make no friends. A spoonful of honey will catch more flies than a gallon of vinegar.
Benjamin Franklin, statesman

Get your facts first and then you can distort them as much as you wish.
Mark Twain, writer

Talk to every woman as if you loved her and to every man as if he bored you and at the end of your first season you will have the reputation of possessing the most perfect social tact.
Oscar Wilde, writer and wit

Say it with flowers.
Slogan devised by the Society of American Florists

Never relax. If you relax, the audience relaxes.
James Cagney, actor

With good communications there are no surprises.
T Boone Pickens, founder of Mesa Petroleum

The basic rule of human nature is that powerful people speak slowly and subservient people quickly – because if they don't speak fast enough, nobody will listen to them.
Michael Caine, actor

Competition

●●●●●●●●●●●●●●●●●●●●●●●●●●●●●●●●●●●

❝❝ Always forgive your enemies –
nothing annoys them so much. ❞❞

Oscar Wilde, writer and wit

Every company is going to have to avoid business as usual. The only big companies that succeed will be those that obsolete their products before somebody else does.
Bill Gates, co-founder of Microsoft

You can be a very big shark in your market-place, but it's the piranhas which will take you apart.
Sir Iain Vallance, chairman of BT

Competition brings out the best in products and the worst in people.
David Sarnoff, former president of RCA

A man is not finished when he is defeated. He is finished when he quits.
Richard Nixon, former American president

If you have found a way to do something in two steps, you can be sure that someone in the Far East has found a way to do it in one.
Vernon Zelmer, managing director of Rank Xerox

If you are frightened of nobody, you can compete with the best.
Sir Chips Keswick, banker

In business the competition will bite you if you keep running. If you stand still, they will swallow you.
William Knudsen, of the Ford Motor Company

Don't be a sheep. People hate sheep. They eat sheep.
Margo Kaufman, information scientist

Never contend with a man who has nothing to lose.
Baltasar Gracian, Spanish writer

Do other men, for they would do you. That's the true business precept.
Charles Dickens, writer

COCO 'GETS EVEN'...

Never complain. Never explain. Get even.
Robert Kennedy, American politician

If you murder a player, he'll be psychologically beaten before he gets on the table next time.
Stephen Hendry, snooker player

In evolution, nobody gets a free lunch, and the price of being a naked snail is to be doomed to the night and the fog.
Steve Jones, Professor of Genetics at University College London

There's no such thing as a free lunch.
Professor Milton Friedman, economist

Float like a butterfly, sting like a bee.
Muhammad Ali, boxer

Never get into a pissing match with a skunk.
Daniel Ludwig, shipping tycoon

If you can't beat 'em, hurt 'em.
Baseball saying

Consultants

●●●●●●●●●●●●●●●●●●●●●●●●●●●●●●●●●●●●

❝ As a consultant I'm only as
good as the number of times I'm
consulted. ❞ *Ron Pollard, tipster at IG Index*

I come from an environment where, if you see a snake, you kill it. At General Motors, if you see a snake, the first thing you do is hire a consultant on snakes.
Ross Perot, businessman and politician (then a director at General Motors)

I hear they are using consultants instead of rats in laboratories now. Consultants are commoner than rats these days, the technicians get less attached to them and there are things consultants will do that rats won't.
Gerald Corbett, company director at Grand Metropolitan

Changing a business requires dynamite and it's a consultant that lights the fuse.
Shigeyasu Sakamoto, consultant

If it ain't broke, don't fix it – unless you are a consultant.
Winton G Rositer, consultant

If you need a consultant to tell you what to do or how to find it, then *you're* the problem.
Robert Townsend, author of Up The Organisation

Guru? You find a gem here and there. But most of it is fairly obvious, you know. You go to Doubleday's business section and you see all these wonderful titles and you spend $300 and then you throw them all away.
Rupert Murdoch, head of News Corporation

No man can be a pure specialist without being, in a strict sense, an idiot.
George Bernard Shaw, playwright

You don't need to take a person's advice to make him feel good – just ask for it.
Laurence J Peter, educationalist

Corporate Life

●●●●●●●●●●●●●●●●●●●●●●●●●●●●●●●●●

❝ It's always easy to tell a successful executive. He's the one who can delegate all the responsibility, shift all the blame and appropriate all the credit. ❞ *Ronald Reagan, former American president*

BOB HAD SLIPPED HIS 'STALKER' AND
SUCCESSFULLY SKIRTED THE 'SECRETARIES'
PIT' BUT WOULD HIS PARANOIA BE ABLE TO
SAVE HIM FROM THE 'ELECTRIC SPOON'?...

Only the paranoid survive.
Andy Grove, boss of Intel

If you make believe that ten guys in pin-striped suits are back in kindergarten class playing with building blocks, you'll get a rough idea of what life in a corporation is like.
Lee Iacocca, former boss of Chrysler

Self assertion within the corporation is a very delicate thing. The trick is to conform – to know when to blend in – while sticking out at the same time.
Mark McCormack, sports agent

The business world is an extension of the kindergarten sand box – but with quick sand.
Richard F Stiegele, banker

You don't need a Harvard MBA to know that the bedroom and the boardroom are just two sides of the same ball game.
Stephen Fry, comedian and writer

I think if I could create a golden rule of CEOs it would be, 'out after ten years'.
Paul Fentener van Vlissingen, chairman of SHV Holdings

Creativity

●●●●●●●●●●●●●●●●●●●●●●●●●●●●●●●●●●●●●●

❝ The real magic of discovery lies not in seeking new landscapes, but in having new eyes. ❞ *Marcel Proust, writer*

To dare every day to be irreverent and bold. To dare to preserve the randomness of mind which in children produces strange and wonderful new thoughts and forms. To continually scramble the familiar and bring the old into new juxtaposition.
Gordon Webber, advertising executive

Even in the most purely logical realms, it is insight that first arrives at what is new.
Bertrand Russell, mathematician and philosopher

Every act of creation is first an act of destruction.
Pablo Picasso, artist

Only the hand that erases can write a true thing.
Eramus, scholar and theologian

The creative person is both more primitive and more cultivated, more destructive and more constructive, a lot madder and a lot saner, than the average person.
Professor Frank Barron, psychologist

For me, the creative process first of all requires a good nine hours sleep at night. Second, it must not be pushed by the need to produce practical applications.
William N Lipscomb, chemist

Imagination is the beginning of creation. You imagine what you desire, you will what you imagine and at last you create what you will.
George Bernard Shaw, playwright

There is no creation, save in the unforeseen as it becomes necessity.
Pierre Boulez, composer

The more opinions you have, the less you see.
Wim Wenders, film director

Customers

●●●●●●●●●●●●●●●●●●●●●●●●●●●●●●●●●●●●●●●

❝ You can shear a sheep many times, but you can only skin him once. ❞

Amarillo Slim, poker player

To be a truly customer-driven organisation, you must first achieve operational excellence. It doesn't help to love your customer – he won't love you if you don't perform.
Percy Barnevik, boss of ABB

Touch your customer and you are halfway there.
Estee Lauder, perfumer

Treat the customer as an appreciating asset.
Tom Peters, management guru

A customer who complains is doing a great service.
Anon

When you are skinning your customers, you should leave some skin on to grow so that you can skin them again.
Nikita Khruschev, former Soviet leader

The consumer is not a moron, she's your wife.
David Ogilvy, advertising guru

There is only one boss. The customer. And he can fire everybody in the company, from the chairman down, simply by spending his money somewhere else.
Sam Walton, founder of Wal-Mart

Find out what your customers want, give it to them and just love 'em to death.
Jim Maxmin, former boss of Laura Ashley

Satisfying the customer is a race without finish.
Vernon Zelmer, managing director of Rank Xerox

The customer is not always right and we let them know it from time to time.
Alan Sugar, founder of Amstrad

If you love your customers to death, you can't go wrong.
Sir Graham Day, company director

There's a saying in the United States that the customer is king. But in Japan the customer is God.
Tak Kimoto, company director

Do something for his kids. It always means far more to a customer than doing anything for him.
Mark McCormack, sports agent

You should think of your customers as partners, or better still, family.
Victor Kiam, company director

We have a tendency in America to blame the buyer, rather than the seller.
Chalmers Johnson, author

For every customer who complains, fifty walk.
Anon

The closer you get to your ultimate customer, the more you learn about your business.
Victor Kiam, company director

The customer does know what he will need in one, three, five years from now. If you, as one of his potential suppliers, wait until then to find out, you will hardly be ready to serve him.
W Edwards Deming, statistician

Danger Signs

●●●●●●●●●●●●●●●●●●●●●●●●●●●●●●●●●●●●●

❝ When you're green, you're growing. When you're ripe, you rot. ❞ *Ray Kroc, founder of McDonald's hamburgers*

When a company hires an expensive consultancy to give it a new logo and a more corporate image, wise investors often take the opportunity to sell. More often than not, new images are like new headquarters buildings: evidence of the fact that the company's top management have lost sight of their real job.
Tim Jackson, journalist

Those who have long drives tend to be out of touch.
Lord Tebbitt, former Conservative Party chairman

Watch sex. It's the key to success and the trap door to failure.
Michael Shea, communications expert and former diplomat

It's just when you are most successful that you are most vulnerable. That is when you make your biggest mistakes.
Roger Foster, founder of Apricot Computers

People idolise authority figures, so senior executives tend to get surrounded by liars.
Professor Manfred Ket de Vries, psychoanalyst and management teacher

When the mom and pop liquor store on the corner is going public and all the university students want to work on the market or ordinary people are giving up their day jobs to 'dabble' – that's when to get out.
Jim Rogers, investment guru

He who stands on tiptoe does not stand firm.
Lao-Tzu, philosopher

Chains of habit are too light to be felt until they are too heavy to be broken.
Warren Buffett, investment guru

A big shot who has never laid an egg – in his insulated opinion – is in the position of a hen under a similar handicap, about to be made a meal of.
Malcolm Forbes, publisher

The ultimate risk is not taking a risk.
Sir James Goldsmith, industrialist and politician

Don't get high on your own supply.
Saying

Risk comes from not knowing what you are doing.
Warren Buffett, investment guru

A sure sign of frustration is putting on weight. Watch for it on the people who work for you. Remove the cause and the weight will come back off.
Robert Townsend, author of Up the Organisation

The bigger the headquarters, the more decadent the company.
Sir James Goldsmith, industrialist and politician

Rolls Royces with personalised number plates; a fountain in the reception area; a flag pole; the Queen's award for industry (UK companies only); a chairman who is honoured for his services to industry – every industry but his own; a salesman or engineer as chief executive; a recent move into modern offices.
Bill Mackey, insolvency practitioner

Sell the shares when the chairman or chief executive becomes president of the C.B.I.
Sir Mark Weinberg, company director

Deals

● ●

❝ When your opponent's sitting there holding all the aces, there's only one thing to do: kick over the table. ❞

Dean Martin, actor

A thing well bought is half sold.
Rudolph Palumbo, property developer

A manager must buy cheap and sell dear. Another manager rings me to ask about a player. 'He's great,' I say, 'super lad, goes to church twice a day, good in the air, make a great son-in-law.' You never tell them he couldn't trap a bag of cement.
Tommy Docherty, football manager

A bad agreement is better than a good lawyer.
Italian proverb

The best deals never stand up to moral scrutiny.
Aristotle Onassis, shipping tycoon

Contracts are made to be broken, but a handshake is the law of God.
J R Ewing, television character in the series Dallas

If you are going to bluff, make it a big one.
Amarillo Slim, poker player

To begin to think, is to begin to make deals.
Aristotle Onassis, shipping tycoon

Look around the table. If you don't see a sucker, get up because you're the sucker.
Amarillo Slim, poker player

Everything comes to him who hustles while he waits.
Thomas Edison, inventor

Never begin a deal, a battle or a love affair if the fear of losing overshadows the prospect of winning.
Aristotle Onassis, shipping tycoon

Necessity never made a good bargain.
Benjamin Franklin, statesman

If you think a deal you are being offered is too good to be true, it probably is.
Sir David Walker, former chairman of the Securities and Investment Board

Remember there are no bargains.
Anon

The buyer needs a hundred eyes, the seller just one.
George Herbert, poet

There's a sucker born every minute.
P T Barnum, American showman

Take care to sell your horse before he dies. The art of life is passing losses on.
Robert Frost, poet

I learned that when you're arriving in New York or Los Angeles, about half an hour before you arrive, you need to go into the bathroom and put on a Rambo outfit: the flamethrower, the camouflage, a knife between your teeth. You get off the plane like that, and that's how you need to be all the time you're there. Because otherwise, they'll kill you.
Mickie Most, record producer

It is wise to remember that you are one of those who can be fooled some of the time.
Laurence J Peter, educationalist

A business deal should not be a win/lose contest but rather should be an effort to seek an arrangement which has something in it for everyone. Without that the deal will not endure. Business is not about one-off deals. It is about building relationships.

Sir John Harvey-Jones, former chairman of I.C.I.

For me a deal without cash is like a kiss without pash.

Christopher Moran, former Lloyd's underwriter

Debt

∙∙∙∙∙∙∙∙∙∙∙∙∙∙∙∙∙∙∙∙∙∙∙∙∙∙∙∙∙∙∙∙∙∙

❝ Never call a man a fool. Borrow from him. ❞ *Addison Mizner, architect*

Creditors have better memories than debtors.
Benjamin Franklin, statesman

If you laugh when you borrow, you'll cry when you pay.
Jewish saying

When you combine ignorance with leverage, you get some pretty interesting results.
Warren Buffett, investment guru

Pay every debt as if God wrote the bill.
Ralph Waldo Emerson, essayist and poet

Borrowed garments never fit well.
Proverb

If you have no money, be polite.
Danish proverb

Lend money to an enemy and thou'lt gain him; to a friend and thou'lt lose him.
Benjamin Franklin, statesman

Decisions

● ●

❝ In every success story, you find someone who made a courageous decision. ❞ *Peter Drucker, management guru*

Never make a decision until you have to, because often they are made for you.
Bill Shankly, football manager

Make every decision as if you owned the whole company.
Robert Townsend, author of Up the Organisation

Rise and fall by your own decisions or get out.
Alan Sugar, founder of Amstrad

It is better to take action, make mistakes and be forgiven, than to wait and ask for permission.
Bill Gates, co-founder of Microsoft

If you can't make decisions in this game, if you can't make decisions in life, you're a bloody menace. You'd do better to go and be an MP.
Bill Shankly, football manager

All decisions should be made as low as possible in the organisation. The Charge of the Light Brigade was ordered by an officer who wasn't there looking at the territory.
Robert Townsend, author of Up the Organisation

Once you have made a decision, never explain, never apologise.
Lord Scanlon, trade union leader

Persuade the decision-takers that the decision you want is their idea.
Michael Shea, communications expert and former diplomat

Urgency should be deliberate and executed with patience.
Captain Picard, captain of the Starship Enterprise in the television programme Star Trek

It is harder to change a decision than to make one.
Anon

Good judgement is the result of experience, and experience is the result of bad judgement.
Walton Wriston, banker

If you empower dummies, you get bad decisions faster.
Richard Teerlink, chief executive officer of Harley-Davidson

Passion persuades more than intellectual debate.
Anita Roddick, co-founder of The Body Shop

No man's judgement is better than his information.
George F Getty, father of John Paul Getty

We know what happens to people who stay in the middle of the road. They get run down.
Aneurin Bevan, politician

When you have them by the balls, their hearts and minds will follow.
Charles Colson, former aide to President Nixon

Economists

••••••••••••••••••••••••••••••••••

" There are three kinds of economists:
those who can count and those who
can't. " *Eddie George, governor of the Bank of England*

Where two or three economists are gathered together, there are four or five opinions.
Anon

In economics the basic questions do not change – it is the answers that change from time to time.
Anon

It would be a dreadful mistake to equate economics with real life.
Sir Peter Middleton, civil servant

The first law of economics is that when the price goes up, consumption goes down. This is a divine law. You cannot change it.
Sheikh Ahmed Yamani, former Saudi oil minister

Economists are people who work with numbers but don't have the personality to be accountants.
Anon

Economics is extremely useful as a form of employment for economists.
John Kenneth Galbraith, economist

A love of fashion makes the economy go round.
Liz Tilberis, journalist

Employees

●●●●●●●●●●●●●●●●●●●●●●●●●●●●●●●●●●●

66 Pay your people the least possible
and you'll get from them the same. 99

Malcolm Forbes, founder of Forbes *magazine*

Treat employees like partners, and they act like partners.
Fred Allen, chairman of Pitney-Bowes

The ability to handle people is a commodity that can be bought like sugar and coffee.
John D Rockefeller, American industrialist

In a hierarchy every employee tends to rise to his level of incompetence.
Laurence J Peter, educationalist

If a human being is condemned and restricted to perform the same function over and over again, he will not even be a good ant, not to mention a good human.
Norbert Wiener, mathematician

People are a resource and not a cost.
Peter Drucker, management guru

If you want to be prosperous for a year, grow grain. If you want to be prosperous for ten years, grow trees. If you want to be prosperous for a lifetime, grow people.
Anon

How we manage people is going to be one of the most significant competitive advantages a business can have, because the traditional competitive advantages – where you manufacture and where you are headquartered – have eroded.
Dr Edward Lawler III, management guru

Everyone contributes. We expect every staff member to carry a rifle. Either you are making an input, or you are output.
Lord Sheppard, former chairman of Grand Metropolitan

If you humiliate people publicly, they may support you publicly. But they will hate you in private.
General Vernon Walters, American soldier

Enemies

● ●

❝ Better to have your enemies inside the tent pissin' out than outside pissin' in. ❞ *Lyndon Johnson, former American president*

Hug your friends tight, but your enemies tighter – hug them so tight they can't wiggle.
Lyndon Johnson, former American president

Never attack an opponent when he is killing himself.
Gerald Kaufman, MP

Always assume your opponent to be smarter than you.
Walter Rathenau, German industrialist

Keep your friends close, but your enemies closer.
Sicilian saying

Money doesn't buy friends but it allows a better class of enemy.
Spike Milligan, comedian

Forgive your enemies, but never forget their names.
John F Kennedy, former American president

Friends may come and go but enemies accumulate.
Dr Thomas Jones, scientist

If you want to make enemies, try to change something.
Woodrow Wilson, former American president

A dead enemy always smells good.
Alus Vitellius, Roman emperor

Everything which the enemy least expect will succeed the best.
King Frederick II of Prussia

Don't make an enemy out of anyone you have sex with.
Psychologist

Be so subtle that you are invisible. Be so mysterious that you are intangible. Then you will control your rival's fate.
Sun Tzu, philosopher

He that is taken and put into prison is not conquered, though overcome, for he is still an enemy.
Thomas Hobbes, philosopher

Failure

• •

❝ Failure is the opportunity to begin again more intelligently. ❞ *Henry Ford,*

motor manufacturer

Failure is inevitable. Success is elusive.
Steven Spielberg, film director

A man is a business failure if he lets his family life interfere
with his business record.
John Paul Getty, oil tycoon

A beaten general is disgraced forever.
Marshal Ferdinand Foch, soldier

A defeated man does not make a good philosopher.
Jean Dutourd, historian

Ignore all the statistics that tell you that 95 per cent of all
new businesses fail in the first eight years. Not only are
these 'statistics' riddled with widely wrong assumptions
and false failure rates, but they don't apply to you.
Dwelling on the statistics is like staying up to study divorce
rates on your wedding night.
Paul Dickson, business writer

Never accept failure, no matter how often it visits you.
Keep on going. Never give up. Never.
Dr Michael Smurfit, chairman and chief executive of Smurfit

If all else fails, immortality can always be assured by
spectacular error.
Professor John Kenneth Galbraith, economist

It's important to have a good failure when you are young.
Walt Disney, film producer

The seeds of every company's demise are contained in its
business plan.
Fred Adler, company director

Men don't plan to fail, they fail to plan.
William J Siegel, company director

Failure is the condiment that gives success its flavour.
Truman Capote, writer

Failures are like skinned knees – painful but superficial.
Ross Perot, businessman and politician

Success is not a harbor [sic] but a voyage with its own perils
to the spirit. The game of life is to come up a winner, to
be a success or to achieve what we set out to do. Yet there
is always the danger of failing as a human being. The lesson
that most of us on this voyage never learn, but can never
quite forget, is that to win is sometimes to lose.
Richard Nixon, former American president

Failure will give you new ideas. You know, I always say,
'the most stupid farmer has the biggest potato'.
Paul Fentener van Vlissingen, chairman of SHV Holdings

There are a hundred thousand reasons for failure but not
a single excuse.
Alfred E Lyon, the former chairman of Philip Morris

If you think you can't, you're right, you can't.
Henry Ford, motor manufacturer

Bad luck is because of bad planning, bad execution, bad
preparation – bad attention to detail.
Jackie Stewart, former motor racing driver

The secret is to be arrogant in defeat and humble in victory.
Ken Bates, chairman of Chelsea FC

The next best thing to playing and winning is playing and
losing.
Nick the Greek, poker player

The man who complains about the way the ball bounces
is likely to be the one who dropped it.
Lou Holtz, American football coach

If at first you don't succeed, destroy all the evidence that you tried.

Anon

Capitalism without bankruptcy is like Christianity without Hell.

Frank Borman, airline executive

Friends

●●●●●●●●●●●●●●●●●●●●●●●●●●●●●●●●●

❝ Your friend is the man who knows
all about you and still likes you. ❞

Elbert Hubbard, writer

A friendship founded on business is better than a business founded on friendship.
John D Rockefeller, American industrialist

All things being equal, people will buy from a friend. All things being not so equal, people will *still* buy from a friend.
Mark McCormack, sports agent

You learn in this business: if you want a friend get a dog.
Carl Icahn, takeover specialist

Always remember, yesterday's enemy is very often tomorrow's friend.
Tiny Lonrho, former chief executive of Lonrho

You're never alone with a cue.
Alex Higgins, snooker player

You can make more friends in two months by becoming interested in other people, than you can in two years by trying to get people interested in you.
Dale Carnegie, motivator

You have to be ready to carry your cross if you want to become the head of a large business. You'll lose many of your friends along the way.
Ray Kroc, founder of McDonald's hamburgers

Business, you know, may bring money, but friendship hardly ever does.
Jane Austen, writer

Friction

●●●●●●●●●●●●●●●●●●●●●●●●●●●●●●●●●●

❝ Anyone can become angry – that is easy. But to be angry with the right person, to the right degree, for the right purpose, at the right time and in the right way – this is not easy. ❞

Aristotle, philosopher

He who wields the knife, never wears the crown.
*Michael Heseltine, MP, unsuccessful candidate for the leadership of
the Conservative Party.*

Don't be afraid of friction. Friction is the mother of progress
and the stimulus for aggressiveness. If you fear friction,
you will become servile and timid.
Hideo Yoshida, then president of Dentsu

When you're angry, never put it in writing.
Estee Lauder, perfumer

It is better to be feared than loved, if you cannot be both.
Machiavelli, philosopher

Never forget what a man says when he is angry.
Henry Ward Beecher, American preacher

Virility is an illness which is best avoided.
*Sir Nicholas Goodison, former chairman of the London Stock
Exchange*

A sneer pushes you on like anything.
Sir Terence Conran, designer

The Future

••••••••••••••••••••••••••••••••••

66 The future ain't what it used to
be. 99 *Yogi Berra, baseball manager*

The best way to predict the future is to invent it.
John Sculley, former boss of Apple

The best way to prepare for the future is to have some optimism about it. Doomsayers don't prepare for the future well.
Kevin Kelly, Big Think guy at Wired *magazine*

Someone's sitting in the shade today because someone planted a tree a long time ago.
Warren Buffett, investment guru

Anyone who thinks they can tell you where a business will be in five years' time is talking nonsense.
Alan Sugar, founder of Amstrad

If you want to do your children a favour, have them learn Chinese.
Jim Rogers, investment guru

Control your destiny or someone else will.
Jack Welch, boss of GE

Don't try to innovate for the future. Innovate for the present.
Peter Drucker, management guru

The rule on staying alive as a forecaster is to give 'em a number or give 'em a date, but never give 'em both at once.
Jane Bryant Quinn, business writer

One doesn't get to the future first by letting someone else blaze the trail.
Gary Hamel, business guru

The childhood shows the man, as morning shows the day.
John Milton, poet

The successful executive of the next Millennium will have to realise that money and information are not national and are totally out of control of any political system we have, but – above all – he will have to realise that what happens in the most remote corner of the world may tomorrow have an impact on his own local market; he should realise that already there is no economic centre.
Peter Drucker, management guru

In business, like the martial arts, the essential thing is not just to deflect blows, but to foresee where they are coming from.
Bernard Tapie, French businessman

Hiring and Firing

●●●●●●●●●●●●●●●●●●●●●●●●●●●●●●●

❝ If you're not fired with enthusiasm,
you'll be fired with enthusiasm. ❞

Vince Lombardi, coach

Hire an attitude, train a skill.
Chris Lewis, business writer

Hiring people is similar to buying a tie. You don't buy the tie when you need one. You buy the tie when you see one and like it.
Henry Grunfeld, co-founder of S.G. Warbug

✗ Time spent on hiring is time well spent.
Andy Grove, boss of Intel

If you've got three Scots in your side, you've got a chance of winning something. If you've got any more, you're in trouble.
Bill Shankly, football manager

You hire people who are brighter than yourself, pinch their ideas and remember to say thank you.
David Rowland, chairman of Lloyd's of London

I always say to executives that they ought to go and see *King Lear*, because they'll be out there too one day, wandering on the heath without a company car.
Professor Charles Handy, social philosopher

Ruthless in decision, considerate in action.
Jim Slater, investment writer

If each of us hires people who are smaller than we are, we shall become a company of dwarfs. But if each of us hires people who are bigger than we are, we shall become a company of giants.
David Ogilvy, advertising guru

Never hire someone who knows less than you about what he was hired to do.
Malcolm Forbes, founder of Forbes *magazine*

Never send a man to do a horse's job.
Mr Ed, the talking horse from the 1960s television series of the same name

It doesn't matter to me if a man is from Harvard or Sing Sing. We hire the man, not the history.
Henry Ford, motor manufacturer

You can only pick people you have been through the shadow of death with.
Sir Bob Scholey, then chairman of British Steel

Someone once said that in looking for people to hire, you look for three qualities: integrity, intelligence and energy. And if they don't have the first, the other two will kill you. You think about it, it's true. If you hire someone without the first, you really want them to be dumb and lazy.
Warren Buffett, investment guru

Credentials are not the same as accomplishments.
Rolf Half, consultant

Don't hire anybody over 35 years old with ten or more years in a big union. It's not worth the effort to turn them round so they're working for you instead of against you.
Robert Townsend, author of Up The Organisation

Don't hire people to do things you can contract out, because contractors don't require stock options.
Robert X Cringely, writer

All you need is a bag of nickels and a phone book and you're a headhunter.
Sid Wilkins, headhunter

I want a man who'll go through a wall of fire with his leg broken and come out the other end still shooting for goal.
Bill Shankly, football manager

Hire people of youth and vitality, people who are chronic grumblers about the status quo.
Warren Bennis, business guru

The heavier the culling the fitter the herd.
Saying

A sexy looking woman is definitely going to get a longer interview, but she won't get the job.
Thomas Cash, psychologist

Always dress for the job you want rather than the one you've already got.
Dr David Lewis, psychologist

Employ a teenager while he still knows everything.
Graffiti

If you are a president who fires people, you will be remembered for that long after you die.
Kazuo Nukazawa, managing director of Keidanren, Japan's leading business council

Ideas

●●●●●●●●●●●●●●●●●●●●●●●●●●●●●●●●●●●

❝ We think too small. Like the frog at the bottom of the well. He thinks the sky is only as big as the top of the well. If he surfaced, he would have an entirely different view. ❞ *Mao Tse-Tung,*

Chinese politician

If they haven't heard it before, it's original.
Gene Fowler, writer

Even truth needs to be clad in new garments if it is to appeal to a new age.
G C Lichtenberg, physicist and philosopher

Beware new fashions. When many people go after the same business, collective imprudence is the result. Too many people after the same business means a deterioration of quality and elimination of profit margins. Fashions carry the seeds of their own destruction.
Sir Martin Jacomb, banker

Ideas are somewhat like babies – they are born small, immature and shapeless. They are promise rather than fulfilment. In the innovative company executives do not say, 'This is a damn-fool idea'. Instead they ask, 'What would be needed to make this embryonic, half-baked, foolish idea into something that makes sense, that is an opportunity for us?'
Peter Drucker, management guru

You can resist an invading army; you cannot resist an idea whose time has come.
Victor Hugo, writer

The centre of a company should have lots of fantasies. It should be a man or a woman with impossible dreams and incredible visions that he or she cannot rationalise and can't get out of computers. He or she should have this idea that something can be done somewhere, somehow.
Paul Fentener van Vlissingen, chairman SHV Holdings

Ideas are one of the few ways to gain a real competitive advantage.
Marvin Bower, consultant

The idea precedes the deed.
Theodore Levitt, management guru

Imagination is more important than knowledge.
Albert Einstein, scientist

When all think alike, no one thinks very much.
Walter Lipmann, journalist

Investment

●●●●●●●●●●●●●●●●●●●●●●●●●●●●●●●●●●

❝ One of the things investors have
learned about emerging markets
recently is that they are hard to emerge
from in an emergency. ❞ *Robert Hormats of*

Goldman Sachs

Buy stocks like you buy your groceries, not like you buy your perfume.
Warren Buffett, investment guru

October is one of the worst months to play the stock exchange. Other bad months are July, January, September, April, November, May, March, June, December, August and February.
Mark Twain, writer

Rule number one: never lose money. Rule number two: never forget rule number one.
Warren Buffett, investment guru

I always say buy a snake for your children and ten years later when they leave home it'll be worth a lot more. You never lose money on snakes.
Robert Snowdon, reptile lover

Investment is like marriage. It involves commitment and adjustment.
Alvin Hall, investment advisor

Buy to the sound of the cannon; sell to the sound of the violins.
Anon

Most bargains are found near the point of maximum pessimism.
Sir John Templeton, founder of the Templeton Growth Fund

Share prices can go down as well as up.
Phrase used in advertisements for financial services

When speculation has done its worst; two and two still make four.
Samuel Johnson, writer

The elements of good trading are cutting losses, cutting losses and cutting losses.
Ed Seykota, trader

Price is what you pay, value is what you get.
Warren Buffett, investment guru

Men who don't take risks, won't drink champagne.
Russian saying

Never invest in an idea you can't illustrate with a crayon.
Peter Lynch, investment guru

Never invest your money in anything that eats or needs repairing.
Billy Rose, theatre producer

Buy on the rumour, sell on the news.
Saying

The dumbest reason in the world to buy a stock is because it's going up.
Warren Buffett, investment guru

Bulls can make money and bears can make money, but hogs just get slaughtered.
Saying

And for God's sake don't invest money with any brokerage firm in which one of the partners is named Frenchy.
Woody Allen, film director

Like Wayne Gretzky says, go where the puck is going, not where it is.
Warren Buffett, investment guru

If you can't explain to a ten-year-old in three minutes why you're buying a stock, don't buy it.
Peter Lynch, investment guru

Rises are very intoxicating, and it's during the period of intoxication that you should be reminding yourself of the benefits of sobriety.
Peter Costello, Australian financial treasurer

You can't buy what is popular and do well.
Warren Buffett, investment guru

When the stock market falls, so does the sexual organ.
Dr Alexander Oshanyesky, blood vessel specialist

The usual bull market successfully weathers a number of tests until it is considered invulnerable, whereupon it is ripe for a bust.
George Soros, speculator

Where are the customer's yachts?
Book title by Fred Schwed, investor and writer

No price is too low for a bear or too high for a bull.
Saying

It's not the answers that make you good in this business, it's the questions you ask.
Michael Price, investor

You must never confuse genius with a bull market.
Nick Leslau, chief executive of Burford

To be a good broker, you need to be able to lie consistently.
Terry Smith, renegade broker

The first rule of venture capital should be: shoot the inventor.
Sir Richard Storey, media boss

A mania is a mania and the experts are caught up in it just as the public is.
Marc Faber, investment guru

Every age in the stock market reinvents the wheel, convinced it has created something new and quite wonderful, while completely ignoring what happened to the old wheel.
Mihir Bose, business writer

There is something about inside information which seems to paralyse a man's reasoning powers.
Bernard Baruch, US financier

People forget that today's junk is often tomorrow's blue chip.
Michael Milken, inventor of junk bonds

If you were going to buy shares or stock in a company, you'd rather have a president who always gives priority to business rather than to his family troubles.
John Paul Getty, oil tycoon

Those who say don't know and those who know don't say.
Anon

Buy a prime freehold site and get the business right. If you don't get it right, it's still a prime freehold site, and you can sell it and kiss it goodbye.
Sir Richard Greenbury, chairman of Marks & Spencer

Don't go broke, go public.
Wall Street saying

It's an old principle: you don't have to make it back the way you lost it.
Warren Buffett, investment guru

Leadership

••••••••••••••••••••••••••••••••••••••

❝ You cannot be a leader and ask other people to follow you, unless you know how to follow too. ❞

Senator Sam Rayburn, American politician

Leadership is the other side of the coin of loneliness and he who is a leader must always act alone.
Ferdinand Marcos, former dictator of the Philippines

Leadership is an action, not a word.
Richard P Cooley, banker

The capacity to create a compelling vision, translate it into action and sustain it.
William Bennis, management guru

Without leadership, nothing happens.
Michael Hammer, mathematician and the inventor of re-engineering

Leadership is something you just have. It is like spots.
Gerry Whent, company director

The question: 'Who ought to be boss?' is like asking: 'Who ought to be tenor in the quartet?' Obviously, the man who can sing tenor.
Henry Ford, motor manufacturer

When a man assumes leadership, he forfeits the right to mercy.
Gennaro Anguillo, Boston crime boss

Managers do things right. Leaders do the right thing.
Warren Bennis, management guru

When are men most useless, would you say?
When they can't command and can't obey.
Goethe, German poet and dramatist

You need narcissism to be a business leader. But when you get to the top, funny things start to happen.
Professor Manfred Kets de Vries, psychoanalyst and teacher at the Insead business school

Leaders must be seen to be up front, up to date, up to their job and up early in the morning.
Lord Sieff, former chairman of Marks & Spencer

Image in leadership matters just as much as, if not more than reality.
Michael Shea, communications expert and former diplomat

Leaders walk their talk; in true leaders, there is no gap between the theories they espouse and their practice.
Warren Bennis, management guru

The first rule of leadership is to save yourself for the big decision. Don't allow your mind to be cluttered with the trivia.
Richard Nixon, former American president

To lead the people, walk behind them.
Lao-Tzu, Chinese philosopher

The function of leadership is to produce more leaders, not more followers.
Ralph Nader, consumer campaigner

They who are in the highest places and have the most power, have the least liberty because they are the most observed.
John Tillotson, philosopher

A company which must hire leaders from the outside, either doesn't hire good employees, or doesn't train or treat them properly.
Raymond Rubicam, co-founder of Young & Rubicam

Leadership is the quality that transforms good intentions into positive action; it turns a group of individuals into a team.
T Boone Pickens, founder of Mesa Petroleum

A leader is a man who has the ability to get other people to do what they don't want to do, and like it.
Harry Truman, former American president

The nonconformist – the leader and originator – has an excellent chance to make his fortune in the business world. He can wear a green toga instead of a gray flannel suit, drink yak's milk rather than martinis, drive a Kibitka instead of a Cadillac and vote the straight vegetarian ticket – and none of it will make the slightest difference.
John Paul Getty, oil tycoon

For just experience tells, in every soil
That those that think must govern those that toil.
Oliver Goldsmith, writer

Losing

●●●●●●●●●●●●●●●●●●●●●●●●●●●●●●●●●

66 The minute you start talking about
what you are going to do if you lose,
you have lost. 99 *George Shultz, statesman*

and businessman

If you never quit, you're never beaten.
Ted Turner, founder of CNN

Show me a guy who's afraid to look bad and I'll show you
a guy you can beat every time.
René Auberjonois, actor

To be defeated is pardonable; to be surprised – never!
Napoleon, French Emperor

A defeated ruler should never be spared.
Stendhal, novelist

Every man's got to figure to get beat sometimes.
Joe Louis, boxer

Sometimes the lambs slaughter the butcher.
Amarillo Slim, poker player

He that lacks time to mourn, lacks time to mend.
William Shakespeare, playwright

Management

● ●

❝ Anyone who would read a management book and treat it as a bible deserves their tawdry fate. ❞ *Tom Peters,*

management guru

The secret of managing is to keep the guys who hate you from the guys who are undecided.
Casey Stengel, baseball manager

Effective managers live in the present – but concentrate on the future.
James L Hayes, president and CEO of the American Management Association

You cannot manage people simply by ordering them around. It does not work and you cannot keep people simply by paying them more money. If you do that you get into the fastest gun in the West syndrome. Someone will always pay more. If you make him very much a part of a team, he will stay.
Michael Marks of Smith New Court

If you can achieve three or four really important things during the year, that is what distinguishes you as a manager.
John McGrath, chief executive of Diageo

If your natural behaviour is to be a bastard, then for God's sake, be a bastard all the time.
Alan Fowler, business writer

Find a kindred spirit in the chain of command and you can reduce the most gigantic and daunting bureaucracies down to your size.
Mark McCormack, sports agent

If I had to sum up in one word the qualities that make up a good manager, I'd say decisiveness. You can have the fanciest computers in the world and you can gather all the charts and numbers, but in the end you have to bring all your information together, set up a timetable and act.
Lee Iacocca, former boss of Chrysler

There are two main skills involved in this job. You have to be half salesman, half psychiatrist.
Barry Hearn, sports promoter

Nice men do not make the best football managers and though there is no perfect blueprint for the ideal boss it seems that a hard, if not mean, streak is crucial.
Graeme Souness, football manager

Perseverance is what makes the difference. You just keep on going, straight on, day after day, putting in the hours.
Gerald Ronson, boss of Heron

Somewhere along the way you have to start thinking of yourself as more than just another competitor. You have to see yourself as a winner.
Dennis Conner, yachtsman

Being constantly curious is what makes a good manager.
Tom Peters, management guru

Good management consists in showing average people how to do the work of superior people.
John D Rockefeller, American industrialist

Management's job is to see the company not as it is but as it can become.
John W Teets, head of the Greyhound Corporation

Managing directors are not paid to be busy, they are paid to think.
Sir Kenneth Cork, insolvency practitioner

He should stand at the window peering through a telescope at the future.
Sir Adrian Cadbury, former chairman of Cadbury Schweppes

There are no bad employees, only bad managers.
T S Lin, Tatung Co.

The master's foot is the best fertiliser.
Dr Daniel McDonald, founder of BSR Monarch

The basic task of management is to make people productive.
Peter Drucker, management guru

Just be yourself, son, because you can never copy anyone else when it comes to the crunch.
Tommy Docherty to Steve Coppell when he went into management

Management is often just watching what happens and either agreeing or disagreeing with it.
Harry Drnec

A good manager is good when people barely know he exists. Not so good when people obey and acclaim him. Worse when they despise him.
Lao-Tzu, philosopher

Managing is like holding a dove in your hand. Squeeze too tight and you kill it. Open your hand too much, you let it go.
Tommy Lasorda, American football coach

A good manager should be a bit of an Al Capone figure. He's got to give his players a bit of heavy protection: from ponces who are after his money and from groupies who are looking for something else.
Barry Hearn, sports promoter

You're only as good as your last two or three deals so there's no room for softness.
Noel Miller-Cheevers, snooker manager

The CEO's job is to figure out what the vision is, not necessarily create it.
Scott McNealy, co-founder and CEO of Sun Microsystems

Most managers manage for yesterday's conditions, because yesterday is where they got their experiences and had their successes. But management is about tomorrow not yesterday.
Theodore Levitt, management thinker

Our conclusion is that, with few exceptions, when management with a reputation for brilliance tackles a business with a reputation for poor fundamental economics, it is the reputation of the business that remains intact.
Warren Buffett, investment guru

The key element in good business management is emotional attitude. The rest is mechanics.
Harold Geneen, former boss of ITT

You've got to be hard to be soft. You have to demonstrate the ability to make the hard, tough decisions – closing plants, divesting, delayering – if you want to have any credibility when you try to promote soft values.
Jack Welch, chief executive of GE

Never leave well enough alone. Others certainly won't, and that affects everybody. That's why it's more important to ask: 'What's new?' than: 'How's business?' 'How's business?' is about the past, but: 'What's new?' is about the future.
Theodore Levitt, management thinker

A company will get nowhere if all of the thinking is left to the management. Everybody in the company must contribute, and for the lower-level employees their contribution must be more than just manual labour.
Akio Morita, former chairman and chief executive of Sony Corporation.

I subscribe to the theory that there's no such thing as bad business – just bad management.
Richard Lee, co-founder of Siliconix

As a successful manager, you need to become a farmer, continuously harvesting ideas from every one of your staff. You need to be out in the field, tending your crop every day, so you can recognise and pick the fresh new shoots of ideas the moment they emerge.
Alec Reed, founder of Reed Personnel Services

When you get to be management, something happens to you. Because when you are down there you want permissiveness and when you're up there you want discipline.
Carl Ally, advertising executive

Lightning rarely strikes managers behind a desk.
David M Kelley, CEO of IDEO Product Development

Wisdom is not the exclusive possession of management.
Akio Morita, former chairman and chief executive of Sony Corporation.

No institution can possibly survive if it needs geniuses or supermen to manage it. It must be organised in such a way as to be able to get along under a leadership of perfectly normal human beings.
Peter Drucker, management guru

In proportion, as any man's course of life is governed by accident, we always find that he increases in superstition.
David Hume, philosopher

Successful management is easy. Failure is complicated.
Lord Sheppard, former chairman of Grand Metropolitan

You don't manage people, you manage things. You *lead* people.
Admiral Grace Hopper

One quality cannot be learned; one qualification that the manager cannot acquire but must bring with him. It's not genius; it's character.
Peter Drucker, management guru

Experts on tap but never on top.
Lord Marks, former chairman of Marks & Spencer

Give a lot, expect a lot. If you don't get it, prune.
Thomas Peters, academic

Divide, conquer and intimidate.
Mark McCormack, sports agent

People respond extremely well to clarity.
Gerry Robinson, chairman of Granada

We took our lessons from King George III. You can't run your American interests from London. He made that mistake in 1776. It simply doesn't work.
Lord White, then boss of the American arm of Hanson plc

Good management cannot compensate for a lack of vitality.
Jean-René Fourtou, chairman of Rhône-Poulenc

Most ideas on management have been around for a very long time, and the skill of the manager consists in knowing them all and, rather as he might choose the appropriate golf club for a specific situation, choosing the particular ideas which are most appropriate for the position and time in which he finds himself.
Sir John Harvey-Jones, former chairman of I.C.I.

SECRETLY FRANK HAD BEEN LOOKING
FORWARD TO MEETING THE HIPPO...

Strategy is like sex with a hippo. It's not a full-time job and
we don't spend a lot of time on it.
Alec Daly, chairman of Anite Group

Synergy, the promise that one and one can be made to add up to three, is the Moby Dick of management: a creature glimpsed but rarely captured, in pursuit of which many a corporate captain has been lured to doom.
Simon Caulkin, business journalist

Sandwich every bit of criticism between two layers of praise.
Mary Kay Ash, cosmetics manufacturer

Marketing

•••••••••••••••••••••••••••••••••••••

❝ Kodak sells film, but they don't
advertise film. They advertise
memories. ❞ *Theodore Levitt, management thinker*

Promoting is not just putting up a poster on a wall saying 'Come and See Nosher Fight Slugger'. We're in the marketing business.
Frank Warren, boxing promoter

When the product is right, you don't have to be a great marketeer.
Lee Iacocca, former chairman of Chrysler

Anyone not immensely interested in people is not going to be a successful marketeer.
Michael Perry, company director

Unquestionably the greatest marketing genius of all time was the unknown insurance warrior who two hundred years ago thought of calling death insurance life insurance.
Peter Rosengard, insurance salesman

Market research is like driving along looking in the rear-view mirror. You are studying what has gone.
Anita Roddick, co-founder of The Body Shop

Communication is the most important form of marketing.
Akio Morita, former chairman and chief executive of Sony Corporation

In the usual and ordinary course of things, the demand for all commodities precedes their supply.
David Ricardo, economist

Markets

•••••••••••••••••••••••••••••••••

❝ You don't buy coal, you buy heat.
You don't buy circus tickets, you buy
thrills. You don't buy a paper, you buy
news. You don't buy spectacles, you
buy vision. ❞ *Anon*

You can't buck the market.
Lady Margaret Thatcher, former British prime minister

Markets never congratulate, they discount.
Anon

The view that the market can do no wrong; is sacrosanct; is your benefactor; your saviour and your ticket to prosperity, is now extreme, as was communism and socialism of yesteryear.
Dr Mahathir Mohamad, prime minister of Malaysia

Losing your lunch now and then is just part of the excitement of being an emerging markets investor.
Mark Hendly, US mutual fund manager, on business in Asia

The market has its law. Were there no law, there could be no centre about which prices could revolve, and therefore, no market.
Ralph Elliott of the Elliott Wave theory

The market is totally impartial.
Anon

I am always fearful of markets and very respectful of them and intend to watch them closely.
Dr Alan Greenspan, chairman of the Federal Reserve Board

The market mechanism is the final arbiter of the soundness of human judgements with respect to economic trends.
Sheikh Ahmed Yamani, former Saudi oil minister

Marriage

●●●●●●●●●●●●●●●●●●●●●●●●●●●●●●●●●●●●●

❝ Bigamy is having one husband too
many. Monogamy is the same. ❞ *Anon*

Trust your husband, adore your husband and get as much as you can in your own name.
Joan Rivers, comedienne

Professional footballers should have more sense than to consider marrying during the season. Anybody who does isn't behaving professionally so far as I am concerned. I've seen so many lads go back a mile until they settle to a new way of life.
Bill Shankly, football manager

Never marry for money. You'll borrow it cheaper.
Scottish saying

When a man marries his mistress, it creates a job opportunity.
Sir James Goldsmith, industrialist and politician

The wife who wants her husband to get to the top must understand that her life with her husband – in the fullest sense – will not start until they are nearing their 50s, and the husband's career struggles are over.
John James, founder of Broadgreen Electrical

Divorce is a game played by lawyers.
Professor Cary Grant, management guru

Somebody recently told me that in Hollywood there's a group called Divorce Anonymous. It works like this: If a male member of the group starts to feel the urge to get a divorce, they send over an accountant to talk him out of it.
Sean Connery, actor

Media

●●●●●●●●●●●●●●●●●●●●●●●●●●●●●●●●●●

❝ Don't tell the Press to sod off. It makes them cross. ❞

Sir Denis Thatcher, businessman

A sound bite won't butter a parsnip.
John Major, MP and former British prime minister

Recognise that journalists are strange characters: loners, anarchic, insecure and suspicious. But they are also gossipy, anti-establishment and entertaining and usually wise enough not to take themselves too seriously. They are, on the whole, good company and add colour to the drudgery of our daily life.
Christopher Haskins, chairman of Northern Foods

When people complain to me that *Private Eye* has left gravy stains on their shirt-front, I invariably advise stoicism. Never answer that lot back.
Lord Deedes, journalist

A PR told me never to smile for newspapers. When your firm makes a loss, they will print your photo on the financial pages with you smiling.
Alan Sugar, founder of Amstrad

It's always best to avoid spear-throwing contests with journalists.
Robert L Dilenschneider, American PR executive

Women prefer tabloids because their arms are shorter.
Mort Zuckerman, boss of the New York Daily News

You can take newspapers and magazines to the lavatory and you still cannot do that with a television. You cannot wrap chips in CNN.
Robert Maxwell, rejecting the notion that broadcast technology would put the print media out of business

If you are going to dump, don't dump a financial journalist if you are deputy chairman of the Bank of England. That's dumb.
Mary Ellen Synon, who was dumped by the deputy governor of the Bank of England, Rupert Pennant-Rea

Whenever I feel the desire to say something critical I bite my tongue and suck on a Rinstead pastille. All the spin doctors should do the same.
John Edmunds, union leader

All mass media have to be at a price of no consequence to the purchaser.
Rupert Murdoch, head of News Corporation

Where possible, the chairman should not hide behind a press office, but speak directly to the press. This disarms the latter, as well as making them self-important. They too, are not without vanity.
Christopher Haskins, chairman of Northern Foods

You know, my Pappy told me never to bet my bladder against a brewery, or get into an argument with people who buy ink by the barrel.
Lane Kirkland, American trade union leader

If you lose your temper at a newspaper columnist, he'll get rich or famous or both.
James C Hagerty, company director

Never let the truth get in the way of a good story.
Media saying

A lie can be half-way round the world before the truth has got its boots on.
Lord Callaghan, former British prime minister

You can say something in a certain spirit, with a smile, but when it appears in print, there's no smile.
Marlon Brando, actor

Probing journalists need to be handled like policemen and lawyers. Offer no more than is being requested.
Christopher Haskins, chairman of Northern Foods

I've looked at the media as allies. Seen that way, you have the entire media working for you.
Tom Peters, management guru

If you say the unprintable to a journalist, it is going to get into print.
Nicholas Winterton, MP

Only mugs bother with blackmail these days. It is much easier to be a bounty hunter for the tabloid scandal sheets.
Joe Ashton, MP

Tabloid reporting is like fucking. You can't learn it at school. You either do it or you don't.
John Mahoney, journalist

The key to understanding tabloids is irreverence. *Nobody* is too scared or important to go after.
Rafe Klinger, journalist

Newspapers are about dissonance.
Dr Tony O'Reilly, newspaper owner

The hip bone should never be lower than the knee bone.
Bruce Gyngell, unconventional television executive, on problems at GMTV

Never read a newspaper at your desk.
Richard F Stiegele, banker

Meetings

●●●●●●●●●●●●●●●●●●●●●●●●●●●●●●●●●●●

❝ ❝ You have to be prepared to have your balls screwed off in public and then joke afterwards as if nothing had happened. ❞ ❞ *A manager at ITT recalling the gruelling monthly meetings which sometimes lasted for days during the tenure of Harold Geneen*

If you're going to have a breakfast meeting, it should be in bed with a beautiful woman.
Lord White, then chairman of Hanson plc

Don't call a meeting in your office – it scares people. Go and see them in their offices.
David Ogilvy, advertising guru

If a problem causes many meetings, the meetings eventually become more important than the problem.
Arthur Bloch, writer

Men

66 Give a man a free hand and he'll run it all over you. 99 *Mae West, actress*

A good man just doesn't happen. They have to be created by us women. A guy is a lump like a doughnut. So, first you gotta get rid of all the stuff his Mom did to him. And then you gotta get rid of all that macho crap that they pick up from the beer commercials. And then there's my favourite, the male ego.
Roseanne Barr, actress

A gentleman doesn't pounce ... he glides.
Quentin Crisp, author

Macho does not prove mucho.
Zsa Zsa Gabor, actress

Kiss a man on his bald spot and he shivers. Lick him and suck him there and he'll go wild.
She magazine report on erogenous zones

A hard man is good to find.
Mae West, actress

At the end of the day you have to look at men like elephants: they are wonderful and fascinating, but would you really want one in your living room?
Marcelle D'argy Smith, journalist

Sex for the fat man is much ado about puffing.
Jackie Gleason, actor

Misbehaving

• •

❝ Quit fouling like a wimp. If you're gonna foul, knock the crap outa him. ❞ *Norm Stewart, basketball coach*

It's better to be a pirate than join the Navy.
Steve Jobs, co-founder of Apple

Anyone who can be bought is not worth buying. I know that now.
Mohamed Al-Fayed, owner of Harrods

Don't steal; thou'll never thus compete successfully in business. Cheat.
Ambrose Bierce, American writer

A thing worth having is worth cheating for.
W C Fields, actor

The secret of life is honesty and fair dealing. If you can fake that you've got it made.
Groucho Marx, actor

Who tells a lie to save his credit, wipes his nose on his sleeve to save his napkin.
James Howell, essayist

Honour sinks where commerce long prevails.
Oliver Goldsmith, writer

A lawyer with a briefcase can steal more than a thousand men with guns.
Mario Puzo, writer

No one ever suddenly becomes depraved.
Juvenal, Roman satirist

A half truth is a whole lie.
Yiddish proverb

No man has a memory long enough to be a successful liar.
Abraham Lincoln, former American president

Men of business must not break their word twice.
Thomas Fuller, writer

The Swiss Wash Whiter.
Zurich T-shirt

If you are a genius, it's a licence to behave badly.
Britt Ekland, actress

Long periods of prosperity usually end in scandal.
Professor George Taucher, academic

Never get caught in bed with a live man or a dead woman.
J R Ewing in the television series Dallas

A man is known by the company he thinks nobody knows
he's keeping.
Anon

You can't con people, at least not for long.
Donald Trump, property developer

Integrity is like virginity. You lose it once. But unlike
virginity, there's no good time to lose it.
*Peggy Czyzak-Dannenbaum, founder of the La Fornaia bakery
company*

Everyone had a good character once.
John Mortimer, lawyer and writer

Money

●●●●●●●●●●●●●●●●●●●●●●●●●●●●●●●●

❝ You've got to move a quid, move a quid. Keep the money rolling. ❞

Alan Bond, Australian businessman

To be clever enough to get all that money, one must be stupid enough to want it.
G K Chesterton, writer

When a person with experience meets a person with money, pretty soon the person with experience will have the money and the person with the money will have the experience.
Estee Lauder, perfumer

Always try to rub up against money, for if you rub up against money long enough, some of it may rub off on you.
Damon Runyon, writer and journalist

Information about money has become more valuable than money itself.
Walter Wriston, banker

Where money talks there are few interruptions.
Herbert Prochnow, banker

Money is like a sixth sense, and you can't make use of the other five without it.
Somerset Maugham, writer

The safest way to double your money is to fold it over once and put it in your pocket.
Kin Hubbard, American humorist

He that is of the opinion money will do everything, may well be suspected of doing everything for money.
Benjamin Franklin, statesman

Put not your trust in money, but put your money in trust.
Oliver Wendell Holmes, author

Monetary policy is around the clock, 24 hours a day, forever. You never reach the point where you shut up shop and break out the champagne. Nor should you.
Alan Greenspan, chairman of the Federal Reserve Board

Nobody becomes a millionaire without a lot of hard work.
Melvin Eddison, lottery winner who was already a millionaire

If you do anything just for money, you don't succeed.
Barry Hearn, sports promoter

Make all you can, save all you can, give all you can.
Lady Margaret Thatcher, former British prime minister, quoting John Wesley, the founder of Methodism

The buck starts here.
Alan Greenspan, chairman of the Federal Reserve Board

Having money is rather like being a blond. It's more fun but not vital.
Mary Quant, fashion designer

There's no money in poetry, but then there's no poetry in money either.
Robert Graves, poet

Money is better than poverty, if only for financial reasons.
Woody Allen, film director

Get money first; virtue comes afterwards.
Horace, Roman poet

More money has been stolen at the point of a fountain pen, than at the point of a gun.
Judge Lance A Vito

Money is in itself, most admirable. It is essential. It is not intrinsically evil. It is one of the most useful devices in social life. And when it does what it is intended to do, it is all help and no hindrance.
Henry Ford, motor manufacturer

If you've got money, you've got human rights.
Yang Jianguo, Chinese businessman

If you accumulate too much money you change, you become obsessive and you are no longer a nice person.
Naim Attalah, writer

Money can't buy happiness, but it can buy the kind of misery you prefer.
Hobart Brown, writer

Bad money drives out good money.
Sir Thomas Gresham, English financier

If you want to make money, go where the money is.
Joseph P Kennedy, American speculator

It is not economical to go to bed early to save the candles, if the result is twins.
Chinese proverb

Never lend any money to anybody unless they don't need it.
Ogden Nash, poet

Nobody works as hard for his money as the man who marries it.
Kin Hubbard, American humorist

To most people a tan in winter means only that you have been where the sun is, and in that respect, sun is money.
Aristotle Onassis, shipping tycoon

If a man runs after money, he's money-mad; if he keeps it, he's a capitalist; if he spends it, he's a playboy; if he doesn't get it, he's a ne'er-do-well; if he doesn't try to get it, he lacks ambition. If he gets it without working for it, he's a parasite; and if he accumulates it after a lifetime of hard work, people call him a fool who never got anything out of life.
Vic Oliver, actor

Money is not an aphrodisiac; the desire it may kindle in the female eye is more for the cash than the carrier.
Marya Mannes, writer

It doesn't matter if you're rich or poor, as long as you've got money.
Joe E Lewis, comedian

Money can't buy happiness but it will get you a better class of memories.
Ronald Reagan, former American president

Just pretending to be rich keeps some people poor.
Monsieur Marc

Money will buy a pretty good dog, but it won't buy the wag of his tail.
Josh Billings, American humorist

A fool and her money are soon courted.
Helen Rowland, journalist

There's no such thing as good money or bad money. There's just money.
Lucky Luciano, gangster

Excess capital is not strength. It leads to the opportunity of weakness.
Michael Milken, the inventor of junk bonds

A talent for making money can imply a lack of talent for leading a useful life.
Everette Lee deGolyer, oil geologist

The place to make money is where the money is coming in.
David Sarnoff, American broadcaster

...AS MICKY THE MINK WAVED GOODBYE TO
HIS MOTHER AND THE FUR TRADER HE FELT
A LITTLE GUILTY, BUT NOT MUCH...

Cash is more important than your mother.
Al Shugart, founder Shugart Associates and Seagate Technology

I found that you overcome all prejudice by making money for someone.
William Bernbach, advertising executive

Cash is virtue.
Saying

All profit is an injustice to somebody.
Aristotle Onassis, shipping tycoon

When the chips are down, money counts more than religion.
John F Kennedy, former American president

People want economy and they'll pay any price to get it.
Lee Iacocca, former boss of Chrysler

Imagine being in control of inflation by curbing the money supply! That is like deciding to stop your dog fouling the sidewalk by plugging up its rear end. It's unlikely to succeed, but if it does, it kills the hound.
Michael D Stephens, writer

Inflation is not something one can go out and shoot and then leave for dead.
Norman Lamont, former Chancellor of the Exchequer

Mottos

• •

❝ Be creative, be desired, be there. ❞

Jean-Louis Duman-Hermés, head of the House of Hermés

England's national motto is: 'there'll be trouble if you do that.'
Sir Alastair Morton, South African born former chairman of Eurotunnel

Make a noise quietly.
Frank George, former chairman of Weetabix

Adventure shrewdly.
Edgar Palamountain, former chairman of the Wider Share Ownership Council

Work hard and say your prayers.
Christopher Heath, banker

Add value or get out.
Lord Sheppard, company director

Be everywhere, do everything and never fail to astonish the customer.
Macy's motto

Leverage your uniqueness.
Bruce Tulgan, management guru

Negotiations

••••••••••••••••••••••••••••••••

66 The fellow that agrees with everything you say is either a fool, or he is getting ready to skin you. 99

Frank McKinney Hubbard, American cartoonist and humorist

Flattery is the infantry of negotiation.
Lord Chandos, businessman

A negotiator should observe everything. You must be part Sherlock Holmes, part Sigmund Freud.
Victor Kiam, company director

Make a suggestion or assumption and let them tell you you're wrong. People also have a need to feel smarter than you are.
Mark McCormack, sports agent

Silence is even better than asking questions if the mood is right; it is always a hard argument to counter. Your opponent will give away his thoughts, approach, opinions, strategy. Talk less, learn more. There is a weight in silence, a great value in an interval in presenting your argument, an influential thoughtfulness in a pause.
Michael Shea, communications expert and former diplomat

Let little things go. Never lose your temper.
Lord Gormley, miners' leader

When money is at stake, never be the first to mention sums.
Sheikh Ahmed Yamani, former Saudi oil minister

A dialogue is more than two monologues.
Max Kampelman, US arms negotiator

Oil

● ●

❝ The oil industry is like a moose trying to hide on a barren landscape. We cannot maintain a low profile. ❞

Robert Anderson, boss of Arco

The oilcan is mightier than the sword.
Senator Everett Dirksen

To operate in the oil business you need chutzpah and luck and raw nerves, steadied with Jack Daniels.
David Thieme, founder, Essex Overseas Petroleum

When I'm thinking about oil, I'm not thinking about girls.
John Paul Getty, oil tycoon

Oil friendships are very slippery.
Calouste Gulbenkian, Armenian oil magnate

Opportunity

••••••••••••••••••••••••••••••••••

66 Opportunities are usually disguised
as hard work, so most people don't
recognise them. 99 *Ann Landers, journalist*

You must believe the unbelievable, snatch the possible out
of the impossible.
Don King, boxing promoter

Chance favours the prepared mind.
Louis Pasteur, scientist

Spotting opportunities is not difficult when you know
what to look for. It's like being a doctor. Once you've seen
a hundred cases of measles, you recognise it straight away.
Asil Nadir, founder of Polly Peck

Look at recession as an opportunity to deliver the death
blow to some marginal players.
Professor Edward Lawler III, management guru

If your only opportunity is to be equal, then it is not
opportunity.
Lady Margaret Thatcher, former British prime minister

There is no security on this earth. There is only
opportunity.
General Douglas MacArthur

Power

••••••••••••••••••••••••••••••••

❝ Being powerful is like being a lady.
If you have to tell people you are, you
aren't. ❞ *Lady Margaret Thatcher, former British*

prime minister

Power only wearies those who don't possess it.
Giulio Andreotti, former Italian prime minister

Powerlessness corrupts. Absolute powerlessness corrupts absolutely.
Rosabeth Moss Kanter, management guru

Power corrupts and obsolete power corrupts obsoletely.
Ted Nelson, sociologist who coined the word 'hypertext'

Power lasts ten years, influence not more than a hundred.
Korean proverb

Power is not only what you have, but what the enemy think you have.
Saul Alinsky, American activist

Power? It's like a Dead Sea fruit. When you achieve it, there's nothing there.
Lord Stockton, former prime minister

There is a power in darkness and keeping things hidden.
Bob Dylan, singer

Silence is the ultimate weapon of power.
Charles de Gaulle, former French president

Apart from the occasional saint, it is difficult for people who have the smallest amount of power to be nice.
Dr Anthony Clare, psychiatrist

If you strike at a king you must kill him.
Ralph Waldo Emerson, essayist and poet

A degree of insecurity combined with a good education is perfect if you want to become a megalomaniac.
Tim Martin, head of the J D Wetherspoon pub chain

Moderation is a virtue only in those who are thought to
have an alternative.

Henry Kissinger, diplomat

Public Relations

● ●

❝ A telescope will magnify a star a thousand times, but a good press agent can do even better. ❞

Fred Allen, American humorist

In matters of great importance, style, not substance, is the thing.
Oscar Wilde, writer and wit

If you give good parties, you don't need PR.
Liz Brewer, party organiser and socialite

Perception is reality.
Donald Trump, property developer

Every time you answer the phone you have an opportunity to prove yourself. Everything you do is an advert for yourself, from how you talk to everyone from the teaboy upwards. Everything is positioning, everything is public relations.
Simone Kesseler, public relations person

Without image, sneer though many do, you are dead in the water. Those politicians and others in public life who think the facts speak for themselves end up in the duckpond.
Michael Shea, communications expert and former diplomat

Price is crucial, image isn't. You can't sell a new logo or colour scheme.
Gerald Ratner, former boss of Ratners

Good PR is invisible.
Peter Bradshaw, journalist

Hype is in inverse proportion to reality.
Tom Rodwell, account executive

It's not what you do or say that counts, but what your posture is when you say it or do it.
Robert Ringer, business writer

AL HAD HAD ENOUGH, IT WAS
PAYBACK TIME...

Can't you get it into your head that it's not important
what you really are. The only important thing is what
people *think* you are.
Joe Kennedy to his son Jack (JFK)

Match your image of yourself to how others see you. Keep in touch with their reality.
Michael Shea, communications expert and former diplomat

An ounce of image is worth a pound of performance.
Laurence J Peter, educationalist

You don't make a dime off publicity.
Michael Milken, the inventor of junk bonds

When the whale comes to the surface and spouts, that's when he gets harpooned.
John Weinberg, former partner at Goldman Sachs

Cultivate what the public does not like about you. That is who you are.
Jean Cocteau, poet, actor and playwright

There is only one thing in the world worse than being talked about, and that is not being talked about.
Oscar Wilde, writer and wit

The fish dies because he opens his mouth.
Spanish saying

It doesn't matter what it is you're dealing with, if you are in the right place, at the right time, with the right message, you can change people's perceptions.
Lynne Franks, PR consultant

You can lead Neil Kinnock to an acrylic poncho but not even Lynne Franks could make him wear it.
The Guardian

Lies and deceit are important weapons and I am the only one who admits it.
Max Clifford, PR guru

Once I'd organised Elton John's Gianni Versace party, I was convinced I was ready. Because after you've liaised with the police and the council, organised rooftop surveillance and shut down entire streets, you're ready for anything.
Aurelia Cecil, PR person

PR is a job for people who can organise anything except their own lives.
Anonymous psychiatrist

Publicity scams are most useful when there is just no substance there at all – in that case that's all you can do.
Magenta De Vine, television presenter

Public relations specialists make flower arrangements of the facts, placing them so that the wilted and less attractive petals are hidden by sturdy blooms.
Alan Harrington, writer

A good spin doctor never gets his name in the paper.
Michael Shea, communications expert and former diplomat

All publicity is good, except an obituary notice.
Brendan Behan, dramatist

For a successful technology, reality must take precedence over public relations, for Nature cannot be fooled.
Richard P Feynman, physicist

A man's reputation is the opinion others have of him; his character is what he really is.
Jack Miner, naturalist

The way to gain a good reputation is to endeavour to be what you desire to appear.
Socrates, philosopher

Bad publicity is good publicity.
Malcolm McLaren, rock impresario

Be funny. Leave the preaching to the rabbi, priest or
minister. Win your argument with a funny story instead
of a sad one.
Joey Adams, writer

If you have bright plumage people will take pot shots at
you.
Alan Clark, MP

I just don't believe that a big showy lifestyle is appropriate
for anywhere.
Sam Walton, former boss of Wal-Mart

It ain't whatcha say, it's the way howcha say it.
Louis Armstrong, trumpet player and singer

The human brain starts working the moment you are born
and never stops until you stand up to speak in public.
Sir George Jessel, company director

While you're saving your face, you're losing your arse.
Lyndon Johnson, former American president

A man who trims himself to suit everybody will soon
whittle himself away.
Charles Schwab, steel magnate

Knowledgeable people know facts. Successful and
prosperous people know people.
John Demartini, business writer

The image you project, in many circumstances, is far more
valuable than your skills or your record of past
accomplishments.
Michael Korda, publisher

Start off every day with a smile and get it over with.
W C Fields, actor

The pheasant that flies gets shot.
Japanese saying

Be liked and you will never want.
Arthur Miller, playwright

Be smart, but never show it.
Louis B Mayer, Hollywood film executive

Personality is to a man, what perfume is to a flower.
Charles Schwab, steel magnate

The day you stop flapping your wings, you fall off the
bloody perch.
Sir John Harvey-Jones, former chairman of ICI

If you're always saying 'thank you', the value of the
currency goes down.
David Ogilvy, advertising guru

Problems

●●●●●●●●●●●●●●●●●●●●●●●●●●●●●●●●●

❝ It's a good law to follow the first law of holes; if you are in one, stop digging. ❞ *Lord Dennis Healey, Labour politician*

If the only tool you have is a hammer, you tend to see every problem as a nail.
Abraham Maslow, psychologist

It's not whether you get knocked down, it's whether you get up.
Vince Lombardi, football coach

In the corporate rescue business, you have to impose yourself. The lions have to appreciate that the lion tamer has arrived.
Sir Lewis Robertson, company director

The fish rots from the head.
Book title by Bob Garratt, business writer

I believe that crisis really tends to help develop the character of an organisation.
John Sculley, former president of Apple

In a crisis situation, speed is more important than precision.
Anders Lindstrom, company director

When business is bad, always start weeding out at the top.
Sir Graham Day, company director

Nothing is particularly hard if you divide it into small jobs.
Henry Ford, motor manufacturer

When the whorehouse burns down, the pretty ones run out with the ugly ones.
Roland Shaw, chairman of Premier Consolidated Oil Fields

To save your company, seek out the anarchists.
Tom Peters, management guru

Inertia is the enemy of progress. Past insights ossify into clichés, processes lapse into routines, and commitments become ties that bind companies to the same course of action.
Don Sull, business guru

Man needs difficulties; they are necessary for health.
Carl Gustav Jung, psychoanalyst

Political turbulence creates a businessman's paradise.
Huang Fu-teh, Taiwanese businessman

If I stop smiling, that's the end of the Thai economy.
Thanong Bidaya, Thailand's finance minister in 1997

If you can't pay off somebody, then that creates uncertainty.
Tariq Banuri, Pakistani academic

Honesty is the best policy, but insanity is a better defence.
Steve Landsberg, architect

Tough times never last. Tough people do.
Robert Schuller, evangelist

The real problem is what to do with the problem solvers after the problems are solved.
Guy Talese, writer

Think of a company like a repertory company. The man playing Charley's Aunt one week, can be carrying a spear in *King Lear* the next. Every problem is new and needs new groupings to solve it.
David Bernstein, founder of The Creative Business

Tough times make people tough.
Benny Binion, Las Vegas casino owner

I have never varied from the managerial rule that the worst possible thing we could do would be to lie dead in the water with any problem. Solve it, solve it quickly, solve it right or wrong.
Thomas J Watson Jr, former boss of IBM

It's good for us to encounter troubles and adversities from time to time, for trouble often compels a man to search his own heart. It reminds him he is in exile here, and that he can put his trust in nothing in this world.
Thomas á Kempis, mystic

When things haven't gone well for you, call in a secretary or a staff man and chew him out. You will sleep better and they will appreciate the attention.
Lyndon Johnson, former American president

Men do not stumble over mountains. They stumble over mole hills.
Confucius, philosopher

When the going gets weird, the weird turn pro.
Hunter S Thompson, writer

If you can keep your head when all about you are losing theirs, it's just possible you haven't grasped the situation.
Jean Kerr, American dramatist

Rewards

●●●●●●●●●●●●●●●●●●●●●●●●●●●●●●●●●

❝ He who praises everybody, praises nobody. ❞ *Samuel Johnson, writer*

People are like dogs; they love praise. If you can't pay more, praise more.
Björn Wahlström, company director

The worst mistake a boss can make is not to say 'well done'.
John Ashcroft, former chairman of Coloroll

You never want to give a man a present when he's feeling good. You want to do it when he's down.
Lyndon Johnson, former American president

People do what they are paid to do, rather than what they are asked to do, so you should always reward ideas.
Alec Reed, founder of Reed Personnel Services

An ounce of appreciation is worth a pound of money.
Sir Ian Bancroft, civil servant

To praise is an investment in happiness.
David Dunn, composer

The journey is the reward.
Steve Jobs, co-founder of Apple

Flattery will get you everywhere.
Jane Russell, actress

Money is not so important as a pat on the head.
Lord Snow, writer and scientist

Secretaries

●●●●●●●●●●●●●●●●●●●●●●●●●●●●●●●

❝ Secretaries will never go to Heaven.
We spend our time telling little white
lies. ❞ *Gwen Cowan, secretary*

You can run an office without a boss, but you can't run an office without the secretaries.
Jane Fonda, actress

I don't believe it is wrong to eat together in the evening if he has no other engagement, but I don't advise nightclubbing. A good brisk walk around the historic sights would be a good outing.
Carolyn Miller, image consultant. (Advice for secretaries on business trips with their boss.)

Firstly, dress efficiently and for comfort – both your own and your boss's; the office is not a place to look either sexy or sloppy. Be friendly without being intrusive or garrulous; your employer probably has more pressing concerns than a blow-by-blow account of your love life. Be understanding without being stifling, interested without being prying, ambitious without being ruthless. Be prepared to think for yourself and if something is making you unhappy, talk it through with your boss. Nobody can read your mind and sulking will only make matters worse … in other words, the ideal secretary–boss relationship is rather like the ideal marriage – based upon mutual understanding and a certain amount of give-and-take on each side. And, in common with a husband and wife partnership, selfishness, disloyalty, excessive demands and thoughtlessness can ruin the relationship.
Margaret Hurst, founder of Brook Street Bureau secretarial employment agency

I think any man in business would be foolish to fool around with his secretary. If it's somebody else's secretary, fine.
Senator Barry Goldwater, American politician

Selling

....

66 Of course, you don't have to use sex to sell things. I have always said that the ultimate marketing weapon is the truth, and I am waiting for a politician to try it. 99 *John Hegarty, advertising supremo*

Work hard, keep quiet, let the customer talk himself into giving you the order. Silence is a very powerful selling tool.
Philip Cushing, boss of Inchcape

The salesman that always gets the sale is selling too soft.
Sir John Harvey-Jones, former chairman of ICI

People don't know what they want until they are offered it.
Sir Terence Conran, designer

You should listen 65 per cent of the time. Thinking about what that person needs to hear to convince them to buy ads with TDI. Being aggressive on the inside but humble on the outside.
Bill Apfelbaum, boss of TDI

Your customers buy from people who are similar. They buy from those who are like them. You can be similar by talking the way they talk and mirroring their verbal characteristics. If their voice is high pitched, then raise the pitch of your voice. If they tend to speak fast then so should you.
Dr Kerry Johnson, sales and marketing guru

Sell the benefit, not your company or the product. People buy results, not features.
Jay Abraham, marketing guru

If you want to sell a steak, you can't just have the sizzle, you gotta have sauce.
Don King, boxing promoter

To sell something, tell a woman it's a bargain; tell a man it's deductible.
Earl Wilson, journalist

THIRTY YEARS IN THE BUSINESS AND
NOT A SINGLE COMPLAINT...

No sale is really complete until the product is worn out
and the customer is satisfied.
L L Bean, founder of the clothing company of the same name

If the package doesn't say: 'New' these days, it better say: 'Seven Cents Off'.
Spencer Klaw, writer

Casting doubt on your competitors is half of sales.
Kip Parent, founder of Pantheon Interactive

The rich will pay anything for quality.
Gucci the First

Give 'em what they never knew they wanted.
Diana Vreeland, fashion editor

Perfume is the easiest product to make but the hardest to sell.
Lois Geraci Ernst, marketing executive

A salesperson's theme today needs to be 'Let me help you', rather than 'Let me sell you'.
Joseph Smith, market researcher

You don't have to compromise your integrity to sell. You simply have to find and emphasise the things that unite you, instead of the things that divide you.
John J Johnson, publisher

Crisis sells well.
Umberto Eco, writer

He that findeth fault meaneth to buy.
Saying

When you have a successful product, it has a life of its own. You don't have to follow convention.
Nolan Bushnell, founder of Atari

The novel is an entry into the minds of our markets. If you are sending a salesman out to Africa or the West Indies, you had better have him read novels. They will tell him more about his market than anything else.
Sir Peter Parker, former boss of British Rail

I don't sell cosmetics, I sell hope.
Elizabeth Arden, cosmetics manufacturer

Stress

●●●●●●●●●●●●●●●●●●●●●●●●●●●●●●●●●●●●●

❝ Pressure is working down the pit.
Pressure is having no work at all.
Pressure is trying to escape relegation
on fifty shillings a week. Pressure is
not the European Cup, or the
Championship, or the Cup Final.
That's the reward. ❞ *Bill Shankly, football manager*

People say that when you start a company you don't sleep at night, but if you start one in a recession, you don't even go to bed.
John Banks, advertising executive

If you can't keep up, drag them down to your level.
Laurence J Peter, educationalist

If you can play as if it means nothing when it means everything, you've got it.
Steve Davis, snooker player

Scar tissue forms on boxers' eyebrows but in snooker players' minds.
Clive Everton, snooker writer

In any profession if you want to stay at the top you must handle the pressure, it's part of your ability.
George Graham, football manager

Pressure is only pressure if you can't control it.
John Parrott, snooker player

It's like running in a field where everyone is trying to shoot you. Or a minefield. You have to walk like a dancer.
Arsene Wenger, football manager

Rule number one is don't sweat the small stuff. Rule number two is it's all small stuff. And if you can't fight and you can't flee, flow.
Robert S Eliot, heart specialist

Fatigue makes cowards of us all.
Vince Lombardi, American football coach

The difference between success and failure at the top level is less often one of technique than the ability to apply or withstand various types of pressure.
Clive Everton, snooker writer

The route to reducing stress is not to reduce demand on people, but to increase support.

Professor Ben Fletcher, author

Style

● ●

❝ Never speak to a man wearing leather trousers. ❞ *Tommy Nutter, tailor*

Even a pair of underpants can be worn with style.
Gianni Versace, fashion designer

A hat should be taken off when you greet a lady and left
off for the rest of your life. Nothing looks more stupid
than a hat.
P J O'Rourke, journalist

Men who wear turtlenecks look like turtles.
Doris Lilly, journalist

Remember, the City never forgives casual clothes.
Whenever so-and-so's name comes up, people don't
mention the quality of his thought or the pungency of his
prose. They say: 'Wasn't he the fellow who wore suede
shoes to the Bank of England?'
L D Williams, journalist

Unshined shoes are the *end* of civilisation.
Diana Vreeland, fashion editor

Balding is God's way of showing you that you're human.
Bruce Willis, actor

As a general rule it is advisable to have your business dress
say nothing about you – other than perhaps that your
clothes fit.
Mark McCormack, sports agent

It is not only fine feathers that make fine birds.
Aesop, author of fables

Remember you're a star. Never go across the alley even to
dump garbage unless you are dressed to the teeth.
Cecil B deMille, film director

The trick of wearing mink is to look as though you are
wearing a cloth coat. The trick of wearing a cloth coat is
to look as though you are wearing mink.
Pierre Balmain, fashion designer

Shorter, higher, tighter.
Gianni Versace, fashion designer

The apparel oft proclaims the man.
William Shakespeare, playwright

Those who make their dress a principal part of themselves, will, in general, become of no more value than their dress.
William Hazlitt, essayist and critic

The only real elegance is in the mind. If you've got that, the rest really comes from it.
Diana Vreeland, fashion editor

Vulgarity can be positive if it's humorous, tacky and over-the-top.
Koji Tatsuno, Japanese fashion designer

Elegance does not consist in putting on a new dress.
Coco Chanel, fashion designer

If Richard Branson had worn a pair of steel-rimmed glasses, a double-breasted suit and shaved off his beard, I would have taken him seriously. As it was, I couldn't.
Lord King, former chairman of British Airways

Every man over forty is responsible for his own face.
Abraham Lincoln, former American president

Fashion is made to become unfashionable.
Coco Chanel, fashion designer

Success

....

66 When you win, nothing hurts. 99 *Joe Namath, American football player*

If you want to succeed, you have to forge new paths and avoid borrowed ones.
John Rockefeller, American industrialist

It's having the right stuff, in the right place, at the right time – and neither too much nor too little of it.
Alan Sugar, founder of Amstrad

Economic success comes not from doing what others do well, but from doing what others cannot do, or cannot do as well.
Professor John Kay, management guru

Success doesn't beget success. Success begets failure because the more that you know a thing works, the less likely you are to think that it won't work. When you've had a long string of victories, it's harder to foresee your own vulnerabilities.
Leslie Wexner, chairman of Limited, the American retail chain

90 per cent of success is turning up.
Woody Allen, film director

The things that get you to the top are not the best side of your character.
Gerry Robinson, chairman of Granada

To succeed, work hard, never give up and above all cherish a magnificent obsession.
Walt Disney, film producer

Do only what you know best and only talk about what you really know. As far as possible, see to everything yourself.
Steven Spielberg, film director

The golden rule of success is expansion.
John D Rockefeller, American industrialist

Success is something that always comes faster to the man your wife almost married.
Anon

You have to be ruthless, an archetypal thug, that's the secret of success.
Randolph Fields, founder of British Atlantic Airways

Fláming enthusiasm, backed by horse sense and persistence, is the quality that most frequently makes for success.
Dale Carnegie, motivator

If one wants to be successful, one must think. One must think until it hurts. One must worry a problem in one's mind until it seems there cannot be another aspect of it that hasn't been considered.
Lord Thomson of Fleet

I give this tip to any youngster who wants to be a success. I advise him that if he wants to make money he must never think about money. If you are continually thinking in terms of cash you just will not take the necessary calculated risks.
Harry Rael-Brook, the man who introduced the drip-dry, non-iron shirt to Britain

Ruthlessness is not a prerequisite for business success – being harsh and unpleasant is destructive in the long term.
John Bairstow, estate agent

Nothing recedes like success.
Walter Winchell, journalist

Success and failure are both difficult to endure. Along with success comes drugs, divorce, fornication, bullying, travel, meditation, depression, neurosis and suicide. With failure comes failure.
Joseph Heller, novelist

The only place where success comes before work is in the dictionary.
Vidal Sassoon, hairdresser

Winners win. Losers make their own arrangements.
Snooker saying

You have to have total responsibility for winning. It's never fate. It's always you.
Kirk Stevens, snooker player

Success is counted sweetest
By those who ne'er succeed.
Emily Dickinson, poet

The race is not always to the swift, nor the battle to the strong, but that's the way to bet.
Damon Runyon, writer and journalist

Success is a journey, not a destination.
Ben Sweetland, writer

Success is like dealing with your kid or teaching your wife to drive. Sooner or later you'll end up in the police station.
Fred Allen, American comedian

Surround yourself with people with winning attitudes and your chance of success will be high.
Richard F Stiegele, banker

Whatever doesn't kill you, makes you stronger.
Marlon Brando, actor

You're not a star until they can spell your name in Karachi.
Roger Moore, actor

When you reach the top, that's when the climb begins.
Michael Caine, actor

You always have to remind yourself that Delacroix never won a prize, that Cézanne never sold a picture.
Cybill Shepherd, actress

The secret of success in life, and consequently of making money, is to enjoy your work. If you do, nothing is hard work – no matter how many hours you put in.
Sir Billy Butlin, founder of Butlin Holiday Camps

Never forget that no military leader has ever become great without audacity.
Karl von Clausewitz, soldier and military strategist

Battles are won primarily in the hearts of men.
Field Marshal Viscount Montgomery

Winning isn't just about pretty football. It's about hunger, application.
George Graham, football manager

If you are first you are first. If you are second you are nothing.
Bill Shankly, football manager

Coming together is a beginning; keeping together is progress; working together is success.
Henry Ford, motor manufacturer

Every successful enterprise requires three men – a dreamer, a businessman and a son-of-a-bitch.
Peter McArthur, writer

Success is the ability to go from failure to failure without losing your enthusiasm.
Winston Churchill, statesman

If A is success in life, then A equals X plus Y plus Z. Work is X, Y is play and Z is keeping your mouth shut.
Albert Einstein, scientist

The best players are those who can turn indifferent hands into winners through psychological mastery of their opponents.
Anthony Holden, journalist and poker player

The truly successful businessman is essentially a dissenter, a rebel who is seldom, if ever, satisfied with the status quo. He creates his success and wealth by constantly seeking – and often finding – new and better ways to do and make things.
J Paul Getty, oil tycoon

Succeeding in the corporate Olympics means operating under a new, apparently contradictory strategic imperative: to do more with less.
Rosabeth Moss Kanter, management guru

You just have to watch the streets. To stay Up There, you have to stay Down Here.
Shami Ahmed, boss of Joe Bloggs fashion business

The mundane is profitable if you do it well.
Sir Chips Keswick, banker

You never get ahead of anyone as long as you try to get even with him.
Lou Holtz, American football coach

Say nowt, win it, then talk your head off.
Brian Clough, football manager

By the time we've made it, we've had it.
Malcolm Forbes, founder of Forbes *magazine*

Generally the taller the person, the more successful you are.
Tuvia Melamed, management researcher

The conventional army loses if it does not win. The guerrilla wins if he does not lose.
Henry Kissinger, diplomat

If you can be interested in other people you can own the world.
Jay Abraham, marketing guru

Film-making is like spermatozoa. Only one in a million makes it.
Claude Lelouch, film director

One man that has a mind and knows it, can always beat ten men who haven't and don't.
George Bernard Shaw, playwright

It is as hard to stay on top as it is to get there.
Hugh Cudlipp, publisher

Behind every successful man stands a surprised woman.
Maryon Pearson, the wife of the former Canadian prime minister

Size works against excellence.
Bill Gates, co-founder of Microsoft

Taxation

● ●

❝ The art of taxation consists in plucking the goose so as to obtain the largest amount of feathers with the least possible amount of hissing. ❞

Jean Baptiste Colbert, French statesman

People love the words 'tax-free'. It is like saying 'I love you'.
Diane Saunders, independent financial adviser

Oil companies can jump over national boundaries to save on taxes more easily than a kangaroo pursued by a dingo can jump over a fence.
Lord Balogh, economist

An Englishman's home is his tax haven.
The Economist

To tax and to please, no more than to love or be wise, is not given to man.
Edmund Burke, politician and writer

Tax revision is like making love to a gorilla. You may think it's over, but it's only over when the gorilla says it's over.
David Berenson, accountant

Teamwork

●●●●●●●●●●●●●●●●●●●●●●●●●●●●●●●●●●●

❝ If you can't say anything nice about a man, let's hear it. ❞ *Anon*

A little reciprocity goes a long way.
Malcolm Forbes, founder of Forbes *magazine*

Go with the flow.
Ken Kesey, hippie

Turn on, tune in and drop out.
Timothy Leary, psychologist and guru of the drug culture

Don't bogart that joint.
Admonition to selfish hippies

Team spirit is a form of Socialism.
Bill Shankly, football manager

Technology

∙∙∙∙∙∙∙∙∙∙∙∙∙∙∙∙∙∙∙∙∙∙∙∙∙∙∙∙∙∙∙∙∙∙∙∙∙∙

❝ People who have valuable things to say that others are willing to pay money for, will publish in print. Those who have things to say that have least value, the least commercial value, will publish for free, online. ❞

Cliff Stoll, astrophysicist

Software is king, was king and always will be king.
Sumner Red, chairman of Viacom

From what I've seen, success in software technology lies
somewhere between two metaphors; slow buffalos get shot
and pioneers get arrows in the back.
Nolan Bushnell, founder of Atari

If you want to be successful in hi-tech in the UK, first you
have to go to America and be successful there, then you
return home.
Ronjon Nag, co-founder of Lexicus

The chief reason for celebrating the millennium is that
nearly every computer in the country will be put
permanently out of action.
Auberon Waugh, journalist

Avoid the temptation simply to 'put something up there
on the Net'. You'll end up with a business that is all costs
and no revenue. Then you'll run out of money. You won't
be happy.
David Bunnell, founder of various computer magazines

It's the land of the cheap, the home of the free.
Cliff Stoll, astrophysicist

Good software is like pornography: very difficult to
describe but you know it when you see it.
Guy Kawasaki, computer journalist

Treat cash as king because in a digital world cash is still the
master.
David Bunnell, founder of various computer magazines

Silicon Valley is like an individual running around in front
of a steamroller. You can outrun the steamroller on any
given day. But if you ever sit down you get squashed.
Bob Boschert, president of Boschert Electronics

In the world of high technology, it's not what you've got, it's when you've got it.
Jonathan Waldern, boss of Virtuality

I don't see it being more than John the Baptist – not the light itself, but the precursor of the light.
Peter Job, chief executive of Reuters, on the Internet

Information isn't powerful. Powerful people are seldom informed. Who's powerful? Look at some of the powerful politicians. Presidents, prime ministers, generals of armies. They don't sit behind a computer reading stuff off the Internet. Hey, whose got the most information? Librarians do! It's hard to imagine a group of people with less power than librarians.
Cliff Stoll, astrophysicist

Time

•••••••••••••••••••••••••••••••••

66 The trouble with punctuality is that nobody's there to appreciate it. 99

Franklin P Jones, lawyer

The heart of time management, is management of self.
Alec R Mackenzie, time management guru

It has been my observation that most people get ahead
during the time that others waste.
Henry Ford, motor manufacturer

All time management begins with planning.
Tom Greening

If you want to make good use of your time, you've got to
know what's most important and then give it all you've
got.
Lee Iacocca, former boss of Chrysler

Time is more valuable than money. You can get more
money, but you cannot get more time.
Jim Roan, banker

The time is always right to do what is right.
Martin Luther King, civil rights campaigner

Three o'clock is always too late or too early for anything
you want to do.
Jean-Paul Sartre, philosopher

Lost time is never found again.
Benjamin Franklin, statesman

I recommend you to take care of the minutes, for the hours
will take care of themselves.
Lord Chesterfield, statesman

Trade

●●●●●●●●●●●●●●●●●●●●●●●●●●●●●●●●●●●

❝ Fools rush in where wise men fear to trade. ❞ *Peter Drucker, management guru*

When nations stop trading goods, they start trading blows.
Peter Sutherland, then director general of GATT

Protectionism is the last refuge of the loser.
Lord Hurd, former foreign secretary

Export or die.
British slogan

What is a man if he is not a thief who openly charges as much as he can for the goods he sells?
Mohandas Gandhi

The crossroads of trade are the meeting places of ideas, the attrition ground of rival customs and beliefs; diversities beget conflict, comparison, thought superstitions cancel one another and reason begins.
Will Durant, historian

Training

●●●●●●●●●●●●●●●●●●●●●●●●●●●●●●●●●

❝ You cannot be first in industry if you are second in education. ❞

Gordon Brown, MP

Never try to teach a pig to think. It doesn't work and it annoys the pig.
Anon

We should live as if we are going to die tomorrow, and study as if we are going to live forever.
Sir Brian Wolfson, boss of Wembley plc

Professional coaching is a man trying to get you to keep your legs together when other men have spent a lifetime trying to get them wide apart.
Rachel Heyhoe-Flint, England's ladies cricket captain

God helps those who train themselves.
Lord Young of Graffham

Business schools, out of necessity, are condemned to teach the past.
Mark McCormack, sports agent

The mark of the true MBA is that he is often wrong but seldom in doubt.
Professor Robert Buzzell, Harvard Business School

The eggs do not teach the hen.
Russian saying

Creative minds always have been known to survive any kind of bad training.
Anna Freud, psychoanalyst

It's never too late to be what you might have been.
George Eliot, writer

You ain't learnin' when you're talkin'.
Lyndon Johnson, former American president

Having a degree from a foreign school is a lot like having a designer label.
Winxie Tse, Canadian-born Chinese working in Hong Kong.

"...LOOK OUT ARTY, I THINK SHE'S GONNA BLOW!!!"

You can't put in what God left out.
Sam Mussabini, athletics coach

A Harvard degree goes much further in Korea than it does in America.
A Korean-American

A manager develops people. He directs people or he misdirects. He brings out what is in them, or he stifles them.
Peter Drucker, management guru

The best-trained man is the self-trained man.
J Ogden Armour, of Armour & Co

Business schools train people to sit in their office and look for case studies. The more Harvard succeeds, the more business fails.
Henry Mintzberg, business guru

Give a man a fish and you feed him for a day. Teach him to arbitrage and you feed him for life.
Wall Street saying

It's not coaches that make players. It's the mothers and fathers.
Bill Shankly, football manager

Be a Jack-of-all-trades and master of one.
Sir Misha Black, architect and designer

Never mind your strengths, work on your weaknesses.
Bill Shankly, football manager

Wealth

●●●●●●●●●●●●●●●●●●●●●●●●●●●●●●●●●●●

❝❝ When people suddenly become prosperous, they also become preposterous. ❞❞ *Laurence J Peter, educationalist*

The problem with being rich is that you have to sack gardeners. My husband hates doing it.
Natalia, Duchess of Westminster

To get rich is glorious.
Deng Xiaoping, Chinese politician

The prosperous man is never sure that he is loved for himself.
Marcus Lucan, Roman poet

A rich man's joke is always funny.
Anon

They said I was worth $500 million. If I was worth that much I wouldn't have visited Vietnam, I'd have sent for it.
Bob Hope, actor and comedian

The concentration of wealth is made inevitable by the natural inequality of man.
Will Durant, historian

Seek wealth, it's good.
Ivan Boesky, disgraced speculator

Cocaine is God's way of telling you you're making too much money.
Robin Williams, actor

Wealth obviously is not the good we seek, for the sole purpose it serves is to provide the means of getting something else. So far as that goes, the ends we have already mentioned, (pleasure, virtue and honour) would have a better title to be considered the good, for they are to be desired for their own account.
Aristotle, philosopher

If enterprise is afoot, wealth accumulates whatever may be happening to thrift; and if enterprise is asleep, wealth decays whatever thrift may be doing.
J M Keynes, economist

Possessions are called possessions because in the end they possess you.
Janet Holmes à Court, head of Stoll Moss Theatres

Gentility is what's left over from rich ancestors after the money has gone.
John Ciardi, poet and critic

The man who dies rich, dies disgraced.
Andrew Carnegie, industrialist and philanthropist

Women

••••••••••••••••••••••••••••••••

❝ Whatever women do, they must do it twice as well as men to be thought half as good. Luckily, this is not difficult. ❞ *Charlotte Whitton, Canadian politician*

Never tell a woman you didn't realise she was pregnant until you are certain that she *is*.
Anon

Beautiful women cannot bear moderation. They need an inexhaustible supply of excess.
Aristotle Onassis, shipping tycoon

Women are superior. You see loads of bright men with stupid women, but how many bright women with stupid men?
Clint Eastwood, actor

There are a number of mechanical devices which increase sexual arousal, particularly in women. Chief among these is the Mercedes-Benz 380SL convertible.
P J O'Rourke, American writer

Being a woman is a terribly difficult task, since it consists principally in dealing with men.
Joseph Conrad, novelist

Women who seek to be equal with men lack ambition.
Timothy Leary, psychologist and guru of the drug culture

Work

66 One of the symptoms of an approaching nervous breakdown is the belief that one's work is terribly important. 99 *Bertrand Russell, philosopher*

Work like a navvy and you'll be like a navvy.
John James, retailer and philanthropist

Choose a job that you like and you will not have to work
a day in your life.
Confucius, philosopher

If you want work well done, select a busy man; the other
kind has no time.
Elbert Hubbard, writer

Work expands so as to fill the time available for its
completion.
C Northcote Parkinson, writer

Unless you are willing to drench yourself in your work
beyond the capacity of the average man, you are just not
cut out for a position at the top.
J C Penney, American retailer

Our credo is work hard, play hard and don't worry about
the difference between work and play. There isn't any.
An electronics executive in Silicon Valley

The most important thing is the work ethic.
Alex Ferguson, football manager

The harder you work, the harder it is to surrender.
Vince Lombardi, football coach

Nobody does anything if he can get anybody else to do it.
John D Rockefeller, American industrialist

Most people disintegrate morally and physically if they do
not work.
Peter Drucker, management guru

The man who has done less than his best has done nothing.
Charles Schwab, steel magnate

To make a living is no longer enough. Work also has to make a life.
Peter Drucker, management guru

The best investment a young man starting out in business could possibly make is to give all his time, all his energies to work, just plain hard work.
Charles Schwab, US steel magnate

A professional is man who can do his best at a time when he doesn't particularly feel like it.
Alastair Cooke, writer and broadcaster

There is a time for work and a time for love. That leaves no other time.
Coco Chanel, fashion designer

It's the busiest man who has time to spare.
Saying

You have to be efficient if you're going to be lazy.
Shirley Conran, author

. . . and finally

●●●●●●●●●●●●●●●●●●●●●●●●●●●●●●●●●●●●

❝ No call alligator long mouth till you pass him. ❞ *Jamaican proverb*

It is better to be a has-been than a never-was.
Lord Parkinson, politician

The graveyards are full of indispensable men.
Charles de Gaulle, former French president

The great man is he who leaves his successors in difficulties.
Paul Valery, poet and philosopher

That man is a success who has lived well, laughed often and loved much; who has gained the respect of intelligent men and the love of children; who has filled his niche and accomplished his task; who leaves the world better than he found it, whether by a perfect poem or a rescued soul; who never lacked appreciation of earth's beauty or failed to express it; who looked for the best in others and gave the best he had.
Robert Louis Stevenson, writer

The only thing men learn from history, is that men learn nothing from history.
Georg Hegel, philosopher

To want fame is to prefer dying scorned than forgotten.
E M Cioran, philosopher

It's better to be looked over than overlooked.
Mae West, actress

Where there's a will, there's an argument.
Saying

Never kick a fresh turd on a hot day.
Harry Truman, former American president

Never let anyone outside the family know what you are thinking.
Marlon Brando, in the film The Godfather

Trust Allah, but tie your camel.
Yaqub Ali, Scottish-Asian businessman

Never catch a loose horse. You could end up holding the fucking thing all day.
Lester Piggott, jockey

Life is suffering.
The Buddha

Never play cards with a man called 'Doc'. Never eat in a place called 'Mom's'. Never sleep with a woman whose troubles are worse than your own.
Nelson Algren, writer

Never ask the barber if you need a haircut.
Warren Buffett, investment guru

A fat man should not play the concertina.
Mao Tse-tung, Chinese politician

Never go to a doctor whose office plants have died.
Erma Bombeck, American writer

Trust everybody, but cut the cards.
Finlay Peter Dunne, satirist

The only safe pleasure for a politician is a bag of boiled sweets.
Advice given to Julian Critchley as a young MP

I always say, keep a diary, and some day it'll keep you.
Mae West, actress

A man is a success if he gets up in the morning and gets to bed at night, and in between he does what he wants to do.
Bob Dylan, singer

Never trust a man unless you've got his pecker in your pocket.
Lyndon Johnson, former American president

It's better to have loafed and lost than never to have loafed at all.
James Thurber, humorist

It is not *who* is right, but *what* is right, that is important.
Thomas Huxley, scientist

Never be surprised.
Michael Shea, communications expert and former diplomat

Always be a little kinder than necessary.
J M Barrie, playwright and novelist

Never forget that only dead fish swim with the stream.
Malcolm Muggeridge, writer and broadcaster

Anybody who goes to see a psychiatrist ought to have his head examined.
Sam Goldwyn, American film producer

You can observe a lot just by watching.
Yogi Berra, baseball manager

Everyone talks about the weather, but no one does anything about it.
Mark Twain, writer

No one can make you feel inferior without your consent.
Eleanor Roosevelt, American social worker and journalist

Do not confuse the moon with the finger that points at it.
Zen proverb

Two is company, three is fifty bucks.
Joan Rivers, comedienne

Never leave well enough alone.
Raymond Loewy, designer

Follow the crowd and you will never be followed by a crowd.
Anon

When you're not interested in trying new things, that's when you should start hitting the golf balls.
Clint Eastwood, actor

Thine own reproach alone do fear.
Robert Burns, poet

Never let your left hand know what you right hand is doing.
Anon

You don't know what you've got until you lose it.
John Lennon, musician and lyricist

Never drink coffee at lunch: it will keep you awake in the afternoon.
Jilly Cooper, writer